D0881295

SOME ANSWERS

Malcolm Muggeridge

compiled and edited
by
Michael Bowen

METHUEN · LONDON

First published 1982
© 1982 Malcolm Muggeridge and Michael Bowen
Printed in Great Britain for
Methuen London Ltd
11 New Fetter Lane, London EC4P 4EE
by Redwood Burn Ltd
Trowbridge, Wiltshire

British Library Cataloguing in Publication Data

Muggeridge, Malcolm
    Some answers.
    I. Title   II. Bowen, Michael
    082   PR6063.U/

    ISBN 0–413–49940–5

Contents

Introduction

It was in July 1950 that I first went on *Any Questions?*, one of the BBC's longest-running radio programmes; thenceforth from time to time, though sometimes with longish gaps when I happened to be in disgrace in Broadcasting House for one reason or another. When Michael Bowen, the programme's illustrious producer for twenty-five years and now retired, suggested making an anthology culled from my contributions, I readily agreed. The proposal was flattering, and anyway old superannuated journalists like myself find it difficult to resist any suggestion for using words already written or spoken rather than having to produce new ones – a labour that in old age grows ever more arduous.

The result, when it came into my hands, I must say appalled me somewhat; being suddenly confronted with one's off-the-cuff opinions on all sorts of topics over the years is quite a chastening experience. We write words with due consideration, altering them and re-arranging them to get them just right, but speak them carelessly on the assumption that, once uttered, they will go with the wind and be lost for ever. Now technology has altered all that, making it possible for words carelessly spoken on an *Any Questions?* programme to be as everlasting as the Tables of the Law that Moses brought down from his encounter with God on Mount Sinai. A terrifying thought!

Going through the extracts from *Any Questions?* programmes that Michael Bowen has put together, I note that my opinion on such matters as death with dignity and factory farming, Women's Lib and Enoch Powell, sociology, television and permissiveness, sex shops and the Closed Shop, abortion, family planning and euthanasia, has not markedly fluctuated as I have grown older. There are, it must be confessed, some repetitions in my various pronouncements – for instance, I never seem to tire of denigrating sociology, doubtless because it was largely invented by Sidney and Beatrice Webb. There are also exaggerations, as when I describe myself as a complete anarchist, or when I say that Marx and Freud enjoy the great advantage, in expounding their ideas, that their writings are totally unreadable.

It was tempting to correct these blemishes, and to trim and prune the extempore spoken words to produce a more orderly and restrained written version. This, however, would have been cheating; holding forth, we all tend to be prolix and repetitive, and attempting to translate our utterances into the lucidity of a Dean Swift or the elegant sentences of a John Henry Newman would be comparable with the efforts of television make-up girls to eradicate the ravages of time on aged visages. So, with just a few trifling rearrangements, the text is exactly as it was spoken.

It is impossible to exaggerate the importance of Michael Bowen's role in developing the *Any Questions?* programme; in finding suitable participants, and getting the right mix in the right place at the right time.* The first programme went out in October 1948, as a peripatetic west country production with headquarters in Bristol. Subsequently, it came to be broadcast on BBC Radio 4, and to roam over the whole country, including Northern Ireland. The set-up has been unvaried over the years. In the centre of the stage the question-master and the producer sit side-by-side, with a microphone between them. When I first went on the

* A full account of the origins, development and record of the programme is provided in a recently published book – *Any Questions?* – by Michael Bowen and David Jacobs.

programme the question-master was Freddy Grisewood, a benign, old-fashioned figure with a bad leg and a melodious voice – he had once been an opera-singer at La Scala. Now it is David Jacobs, who came to *Any Questions?* from *Jukebox Jury*; also kindly, and altogether more contemporary.

The four panellists sit two-by-two on either side of the stage, it being generally understood that those on the left are Leftish and those on the right, Rightish. I am invariably put on the Right, not always to my satisfaction, or to that of the other panellist there, who may well be a Tory MP or otherwise politically orientated. We enter to cheers, and the show closes to cheers, which, I am happy to say, if not precisely spontaneous, are definitely not piped in along with studio laughter as in some radio and television programmes. Being human, we vie with one another for a cheer or a laugh, and occasionally get involved in a shouting match – in my case invariably when I am on the programme with Lord Hailsham, whom I nonetheless hold in esteem and affection.

The panellists cover the whole political, ideological and even social spectrum, ranging between privy-counsellors and bishops, professors and actors, business tycoons, trade-union bosses and landed gentry. Politics and the stage produce the more colourful participants, but by and large not the most diverting; what the politicians – even the liveliest like Michael Foot – have to say tends to be too predictable to be arresting. As for the actors and actresses, the trouble with them is that in most cases they only come alive when they are someone else. This was particularly true of Peter Sellers, one of the great clowns of our time to whom I was devoted.

My own favourite among the regulars was Mary – later Baroness – Stocks, now, alas, dead. In her latter years she developed an impish humour, and one came to realise that inside this highly respectable and distinguished ladyship there was a comedienne of the calibre of Bea Lillie, if not of Nellie Wallace and Marie Lloyd. I made her acquaintance in Manchester when we were both quite young, she the wife of a

Professor of Philosophy at the University and I on the staff of the *Guardian*, and esteemed her ever after. The male panellists were, by and large, in worldly terms a dazzling array. It is difficult to think of a single notability who did not at sometime or other make an appearance on *Any Questions?* On the whole, however, the more notable they were, the more tedious. Of them all, I should plump for Russell Braddon, an inscrutable Australian who has developed to a high degree his countrymen's gift for dry, ironical observations about what is happening in the world and those who direct its affairs.

There seems to be no particular reason why *Any Questions?* should ever come to an end, and I fully anticipate that in the Last Days, when, as has been prophesied, the Heavens unroll like a scroll, somewhere or other – in Littlehampton maybe – someone will be asking what the panel think about the rise in juvenile delinquency, and a clergyman with mutton-chop whiskers and a huge expanse of white dog-collar will be answering that what is required to reverse this trend is more and better education. I shall not, however, be present on that occasion.

Malcolm Muggeridge, August 1982

ONE

Permissiveness, Censorship and Morality

In October 1954 a questioner asked whether the import of horror comics into Great Britain should be banned. One of the team, Jack Longland, the Director of Education for Derbyshire, referred to those 'comics' which exploit the beastliest tendencies of sadism and sex.

It is not only imported comics which exploit these things, and this question of censorship is an extremely difficult one. Certain books lately have led to prosecutions in the courts. These are books which have a very small circulation – they are relatively expensive – and which can be defended. At the same time I am sure you would agree with me that, for instance, a good deal of the Sunday press is extremely unedifying in its appeal.

Now, of course, if you say, 'Right, we will ban imported foreign comics', it then becomes almost logical to say, 'Well, we must also ban things which in fact exploit the same sort of obscenity and sadism which these imported comics exploit.' And so you go on, and you land yourself in an extremely complicated procedure – exactly where to stop, exactly who is to have the final say.

The whole problem, as was pointed out in a very brilliant judgement in the courts recently by Mr Justice Stable, the whole question of framing a law which will cover this question is practically insuperable. I only say that it is quite an illusion for us to sit here and say, 'By all means we will ban these comics and then everything will be all right.' This is an illusion, this is a pipe dream. It would not be all right.

What a free society does in order to protect young and immature people from the exploitation of base things, I don't know. But it is not answered simply by saying, 'We will put an import ban on a certain type of literature.'

In June 1963 there was a question asking to what extent the private life of men in the public eye should affect their position and career. It was the time of the sexual scandal involving the Secretary of State for War, John Profumo. The team also included the farmer Clifford Selly.

It entirely depends on what aspects of private life. I mean, if a man who's a Minister in a government puts his hand in the ministerial till, it's perfectly obvious that he ought to be booted out. Or if he habitually gets drunk to the point that he can't perform his functions. If he can't make himself understood, it would be preposterous to say that he should get out of public life because nobody in public life that I've ever met can, so that if you said that they'd got to get out of public life because they couldn't make themselves clear, you'd simply empty the whole Parliament.

What obviously we're talking about is someone who commits an offence in the sense of going to bed with someone who isn't his wife, in particular circumstances. Of course, one might consider this to be desirable or undesirable or neutral; the general consensus has been that it's undesirable, but it's absolutely preposterous to say that doing this unfits a man for any kind of job, because the great majority of human beings at some time or another do it. And therefore if you're going to say that men who commit adultery may not be Ministers of the Crown or may not be headmasters of schools or may not be this and may not be that, you are going to have very great difficulty in forming a government or finding anybody to preside over the various institutions of our society.

SELLY: *The average citizen leads a fairly tidy life and this is what they're looking for in the people who run the country, and they're entitled to look for it.*

We have to ignore our present rulers because we don't know enough about them, but the statement that you've just made is a statement of such preposterousness in the light of those who have run our affairs in the past about whom, from innumerable memoirs and things, we know a lot. Obviously those people, many of whom were extremely able in their jobs, excellent prime ministers, excellent Ministers of the Crown, excellent viceroys – we know perfectly well that the particular standard that you're laying down did not apply to them. Have you read about Lloyd George? Do you think Lloyd George should have continued to be Prime Minister? Lloyd George, as is well known, was an old ram. It's a well known fact. You aren't seriously suggesting that because he was an old ram someone should have said, 'Step down, Lloyd George; you mustn't be Prime Minister'?

SELLY: *That sort of slander on the Lloyd George family I really think is monstrous.*

But his son's written all about it. You seriously consider that Lloyd George was a monogamist?

Before Clifford Selly could reply, Freddy Grisewood tactfully drew the discussion to a close.

In October 1968 there was a question about the dissolution of the office of Lord Chamberlain – did this tend to lower moral standards and pander to our present permissive society?

Speaking as one who intensely dislikes our present permissive society and is practically prevented from enjoying any form of entertainment because it's so horrible, I don't think that the actual shutting up of the Lord Chamberlain really makes any difference. The plays that are put on are probably slightly more juvenilely smutty than they were before, if that's possible. You have a few more American yahoos invading the English stage and taking off their clothes, but I don't think it makes any substantial difference to the very low standard of the whole thing.

Two months later, Malcolm made one of his public pronouncements to the effect that the way of life of Western man today was the most horrible and degraded that ever existed on earth, and as this coincided with another of his appearances on the programme, a questioner asked if the team agreed with him.

I've never known anything one's ever written or said being discussed without realising that nobody knows what one means. In other words, it's impossible in this world to make oneself clear. You see, I wasn't saying that the world was a nicer place in this century or that century. What I was trying to say was that values today, accepted values, as presented first of all by this Frankenstein's monster of mass communication media that we've created, which we're talking on now – one aspect of it – or even through the agency of education, or even through the agency of most of the churches, the values that are put before people are essentially materialist values. And I believe that the measure of the bearableness of life is to be expressed by the extent to which people find mortal life unbearable – in other words, the degree to which they feel strangers in the world, the degree to which the material values and the physical values of their own being are repugnant to them.

Now, I doubt whether there has ever been a period in history when there has been so little of that otherworldly sense, and so much of this worldly sense – even when it takes the form of a perfectly legitimate and right and good, compassionate attitude to fellow men – I'm not talking about that; I know that in a sentimental way, people today do feel sorry that two-thirds of mankind are starving, getting hungrier and hungrier, while we in our part of the world get richer and richer, and have to invent the most fatuous devices to persuade ourselves to consume what we don't want, while all these other people get hungrier and hungrier. That is the sort of situation that I find both tragic and degraded, and the fact that the only contribution made to it, even by the good, nice people, is to say, 'Well, I'm compassionate; I gave some money to Oxfam.'

In June 1969 there was a discussion about nudity on the stage. The team also included Lord Mancroft.

I think it's an attractive view that you could simply have so much of this that people would get sick of it. But I think you have to be young and romantic to take that view. I have been arguing this for years – that if only there was so much of it, people would get sick of it. Whereas for the whole of my life pornography of any kind has been increasing and increasing and increasing, and there's not the slightest sign that anybody's sick of it. On the contrary, it seems to be in ever greater demand.

MANCROFT: *Hasn't this worked in Denmark?*

It's the most pitiful piece of fraudulence that I've seen, even in a newspaper. What is seriously argued is that in Denmark there was complete licence, up to ninety-five per cent, and then by an Act of Parliament, that was made into one hundred per cent. And the idea is that once they had that additional five per cent of licence, suddenly everybody said, 'We don't want to see any more pornography.' It's the most complete baloney. The shops are loaded with pornography. The real purpose of the thing is, it enables them to carry on a very big export trade in pornography, which in fact these splendid Danes do.

In October 1969 the members of the team were asked whether they thought that, with the relaxing of censorship of films and the theatre, the moral standards of the country would decline.

We don't like censorship, we don't believe in the efficiency of censorship, we have enormous evidence that censorship is a very ham-fisted and ineffectual operation, but we have to face the fact that today, in the written word, on celluloid, and for all I know on the stage, there is a lot of deliberate exploitation for money of pornography of various kinds, and we have to ask ourselves, is this a desirable social phenomenon? I think it's not, and that it is in fact, as it's developing, going to produce the most terrible reaction the other way which we shall all find very disagreeable. All sorts of things are being made, particularly perhaps in films, but we also think of *Oh! Calcutta!*, Mr Tynan's brilliant effort, and so on, that will produce a very ugly reaction. We cannot, though we dislike censorship, defend those statements – they're indefensible.

There was a time when we didn't like 'bloody' and now it's 'We don't like *Oh! Calcutta!*' and therefore those two things are the same. They're not the same at all. There's a great difference between using words which are not usually used in the drawing room and actually using the resources of a medium like the film or the stage in order to develop for money base, pornographic shows.

In September 1971 the team, which also included Denis Healey, discussed sentences for armed robbery.

I accept the view that merely making penalties more severe is not in practice shown to make crime rarer. In fact, you could almost say that whatever has been done anywhere, there is at the present moment in the world a situation in which crime is increasing, and this seems to me to be the case whatever you do.

This business of crime is to do with something much more fundamental than just how we treat people in prison, the sort of sentences they get or even the efficiency of the police forces. I think it is to do with a breakdown in the whole notion of a moral order, that if you don't believe in a moral order – you haven't got the sense of a moral order – you will in fact in time have no sense of any order at all, and this will show itself, among other things, in crime.

Now, Denis quite rightly mentions the bad effect of showing scenes of violence. Equally, the tendency, in a society without a sense of a moral order, to make a hero of the criminal – this also is not without its bearing. And, with all respect to him, when he made this distinction between the pornography of violence and the pornography of sex, I would say that both tend to result in this breakdown of a sense of moral order. Where you have the removal of all restraints upon human behaviour in one particular direction, you may be quite sure that you will get a lack of restraint in behaviour in other directions as well.

In November 1974 a questioner asked: 'This week a private prosecution against an allegedly obscene film was dismissed through a technicality; would members of the team agree with Mrs Whitehouse that the obscenity laws have been shown to be wholly inadequate in protecting against moral pollution?' Malcolm explained that as he was due to be a witness in the court case he went to see the film, which was *Last Tango in Paris*.

This film was wholly obscene. No one could possibly see it without a sense of human beings and our human life being utterly degraded, and that if it continued to be shown, and if in due course as an old film it came to be shown on television, which would be almost certainly the case, this would be an utterly abysmal thing.

Now, on a point of law that case has been stopped and the film will continue to be shown and will almost certainly in due course appear on television in people's sitting rooms. I regard this as a wholly deplorable thing, and it is the case that our apparatus of law provides no protection whatever from this sort of degradation.

My own reaction to it is specifically a Christian one, because in a film of this kind, and particularly in this film, you see the procreative impulse in people – which I regard as the most sacred thing there is, the essence of our whole existence here on earth – you see that utterly, deliberately, for money, for sensation and publicly degraded. I cannot believe that that is a permissible thing, and I cannot accept any argument about freedom or any argument about there being other forms of obscenity which trouble me – of course there are, but that doesn't alter the fact that this particular one is horrifying and that it is a bad thing that our laws do not in fact provide any protection against it.

In July 1977 a questioner asked: 'We have all read this week of the horrific rape of a young girl by boys of fifteen and sixteen; would the members of the team agree that this sort of behaviour may well be the outcome of so-called sex education in schools? In the past we had no such sex education, but young people seemed to grow up with healthier minds and without the obsession of sex which seems to exist today.' The team also included the Earl of March and Elizabeth Longford, wife of the Earl of Longford.

I think it probably has got something to do with that, as a matter of fact. I had occasion, when Elizabeth's husband was doing this pornography report, to look into the question of what was being used for sex education, and it seemed to me to be a deliberate incitement to the young to be precocious sexually. So I agree with the questioner.

I would add that another very sinister feature of this horrible story – and I sympathise enormously with the judge who said that he simply had to withdraw from the court for two hours before he could control himself to issue a rational judgement – another feature of it was that one of the boys, of course, had pornography in his home and that the pornography that he had in his home envisaged the sort of horrible things that these boys did. And it is my considered opinion that our country is destroying itself by fostering this erotic obsession, particularly among the young, and this case was one that was very much to the point.

The idea of permissiveness was that it would relieve the stresses of sexuality. It seems to me that, to judge by what is being brought into court of recent times, as I would have anticipated, it's had the opposite effect.

MARCH: *This particular case probably has very little indeed to do with sex education in schools as such. It seems to me that in a day when contraception is so easy and so widespread, there must be more sex education, and because parents on the whole don't or won't give it, then it must be given in schools.*

LONGFORD: *The sex education in schools, to my mind, fails not because it's given, but because it's given in a purely factual spirit with no moral implications at all. That is no good.*

Would Lord March really consider that the countries in which this sex education in schools is most highly developed are the countries which present the most edifying spectacle – for instance, Scandinavia and California? Those are the countries where you have most sex education.

Of course Elizabeth is right. If you are going to have sex education, it can only be related to a set of moral values, and if you simply teach it as a matter of sexual techniques and sexual precautions to adolescent children, you are in fact inviting them to experiment in those fields.

May I say one other thing in this case that I thought was particularly appalling? These boys had in fact been drinking from pub to pub and they were all under age, so another thing that's happening in our unfortunate country is that laws are ceasing to have any effect whatsoever. That was against the law but they had no difficulty whatever in getting liquor and they had plenty of money to buy it. I would draw attention to those two circumstances to complete this picture – pornography at home, money, drink, at an age when children should be playing games and should be looked after by their parents.

And then this hideous scene, which was capped by the fact that when these wretched boys left off, apparently three adults, who had been watching, joined in. I think it will be in the history books as a sign of total decadence and depravity of a once great country.

In February 1982 a questioner asked if the panel considered that sex shops should be licensed. The team also included the writer and barrister John Mortimer.

I hate and abominate and detest with all my heart and soul the presence of these shops and all they imply and all they signify. I loathe it. And whether it's licensed or whether it's unlicensed, however it's there, it is to me utterly abominable. And being at the very end of my life, I think that I'm watching the final decline of a civilisation when it is prepared to show all these horrible things to be sold for money and trap people into vicious practices, which might be a temptation to them but which, in any case, without all this hullabaloo and these means of doing it, they might be able to avoid. So I don't care whether they're licensed or whether they're not. To me they are the symbol of the decline of our Western society; it's degradation and I hate it.

My dear friend John Mortimer has always steadfastly said that there must be no restrictions because that way you do less harm to people than if you do have restrictions. And the justification has been put to us all for the increasing permissiveness of our society, to the effect that nowadays you will find in a village newsagent pornography that ten years ago would have had to be under the counter in Soho itself. And, by the way, often people speak as though keeping things under the counter was in itself disgraceful, but there are certain things that are worth keeping out of sight, and among them, for instance, sewers; that's just a point in passing.

The point is that in all this business, if it had produced a happy, creative, free society, I would always have disliked it, but I would have said, 'Well, there it is; it has released these tensions.' Actually, in every single field, whether it's raping or whether it's juvenile pregnancies or whether it's juvenile suicides, in all these fields, the figures are the exact opposites: they're all increasing, all the time. In other words, these measures of permissiveness which were supposed to ease off tensions in people and make them behave better are statistically, endlessly making them – particularly the young – behave worse. The whole idea that by liberating people from their morality and from their standards and from their taboos, if you like, you would make them happy and joyful and free – I just say it hasn't happened, and by every single statistic that exists, the opposite has happened.

TWO

Religion

In January 1954 a questioner asked: 'Do any real conversions to Christianity result from the many religious broadcasts?'

I have been listening to religious broadcasts and I very frequently put that question to myself and I think the answer is that you probably just can't generalise. In the morning, very early, you get a religious broadcast and some of them are very banal and some of them are extraordinarily good. And I can easily imagine someone hearing these broadcasts and being really quite lit up as a result of it; similarly, some of the religious services.

On the other hand, I would also point out that the fact that the BBC cannot identify itself with any sort of denominational evangelism – and quite rightly can't do so – may perhaps take the edge off the evangelising fervour of what they do. If I might give an example, I remember driving my car one Sunday in America, in one of the Southern states, and turning on the wireless in the car, and the whole air was full of people preaching with passionate fervour – Negro revivalists, Roman Catholic priests, all sorts of people. Now obviously that would be impossible with the BBC. If you have – as the BBC rightly have – to adopt a position of neutrality as far as religious questions are concerned, it must, to that extent, cancel out its influence with the unconverted. Indeed, it is liable to encourage the expression of neutral views, which could even have the effect of undermining the faith of people who are believers.

I remember in the Ministry of Information at the beginning of the war – there was a religious department there and I asked an individual in it what he was and he said he was an atheist. And I thought this was rather amusing, but of course it was perfectly logical – that if you have a religious department covering all the denominations of all points of view, it is not unreasonable to have an atheist as one of the representatives.

In October 1966 a questioner asked: 'The Scriptures tell us, "Blessed are they who have not seen and yet believe." Can the team give any encouragement to those of us, brought up to believe in Heaven and a life hereafter, who are sometimes inclined to wonder if there is any truth in it at all or if it is mostly wishful thinking?' Another member of the team, the Bishop of Crediton, spoke of the divine sense of purpose in human existence.

All I would say, in the greatest humility, is that even if this is wishful thinking, it isn't necessarily therefore false. I remember reading in some book by a mediaeval mystic that the fact of hunger presupposes the existence of bread, and the fact that human beings, caught up in such trivial pursuits as for the most part we are, engage in wishful thinking of this kind is itself an extremely encouraging circumstance.

Furthermore, I would point out, though it's by no means a conclusive argument, that all the people who have lived in our civilisation for whom we now have any regard, who left behind anything in the way of art or literature or thought that could possibly be of any moment or account, were people who by and large did take the view that the Bishop of Crediton has just expressed, and it's the people who didn't take that view and had no sense of that sort who in fact left nothing that we would care to think of as justifying our civilisation.

In November 1967 the team was asked whether Christianity should be taught as a compulsory school subject.

In my opinion, it shouldn't. The reason is that first of all it's much too important to be made a compulsory subject, and secondly because in most schools there's nobody to teach it and so what happens is that rubbish like mental arithmetic and civics and hygiene get taught in the religious instruction period, and then the children think that's Christianity and they grow up and go out into the great world thinking that all these nonsensical talks that they've had about what a splendid, humane and excellent society we've become are Christianity.

So I would say in view of the fact that there are very, very few Christians in the teaching profession, and that Christianity is the most important subject of all, it shouldn't be taught in schools.

In December 1968 a questioner asked if closed religious orders contributed anything to society.

These monks or nuns are not parasites. They invariably produce their own necessities. They cut themselves off from society because they don't want to be involved in the pursuits of society, which for most of us are to earn our living and bring up our children and satisfy appetites and so on. They withdraw from that in order to contemplate their Creator, to know and love their Creator, and to try and understand what life is about.

Now, I think that to have some people in a society, particularly in an intensely materialistic society like ours, doing that and living in that way is absolutely the salt that gives society its savour. You have to have a shallow, twentieth-century mind to say, 'Well, what are they contributing?' What they are contributing is their own serenity, their own purity, their own wisdom.

I don't know whether any of you saw it, but I was concerned in making a television programme about a Cistercian abbey up in Scotland at Nunraw, and I stayed in the abbey for three weeks. And you must believe me when I say that those three are the happiest weeks I've ever spent, and I have the utmost respect and love for those monks who are in fact living this contemplative life.

Of course, guests are permitted to come to these monasteries and convents, and it was quite remarkable to watch how, just by being there, people who would arrive harassed, fearful, all the things that we are liable to experience in our sort of society, achieved almost immediately a miraculous serenity. Not because of anything anybody said to them, or anything anybody did to them, but because they were in contact with human beings whose whole being was set upon truth, love of God and of their fellows.

Therefore, far from thinking that it would be good that there shouldn't be such communities, I think that if they ever ceased to exist it would be a very black day, and that mankind will always go back to having them, whatever sort of civilisation may emerge.

In August 1973 the subject of religious education in schools came up again. Was it preferable to have religious views, of whatever kind, taught in schools rather than political ones?

What I take this question to mean is whether you should base your teaching on the idea of religion rather than on the idea of politics, which is how people manage their affairs here and now in our society; it really ultimately is about the use of power, that's what politics is about. Religion, on the other hand, is about what life means, what it signifies, why we're here. Ultimately it's about God, and politics are about Caesar – hence the very remarkable sentence in the New Testament about certain things being due to God and certain things being due to Caesar. That distinction in our society has become hopelessly blurred. In general, you have these two aspects of life, and in our society and our education and programmes like this one everything is leaning more and more heavily on the side of Caesar. But I believe every day that I live longer more and more strongly in the side of God. Therefore I agree with the implication behind this question.

In February 1977 a questioner asked: 'Now that Christianity is a fringe activity for the majority of British people, what does the team consider has replaced religion as the opiate of the people?' The team also included the Labour MP Judith Hart.

The questioner is repeating what is the consensus view of this. The consensus view is that Christianity is largely a thing of the past, that it is over and done with, and of course that is, like most consensus views, totally nonsensical. If you look back on the two thousand years of Christendom, the great stimulus through those two thousand years, artistically, in making our way of life better, all the endeavour of those two thousand years which is reaching towards some sort of perfection or betterment of human life, has been stimulated by this Christianity, and it was only that rather foolish old German, Marx, who said that religion was the opiate of the masses.

HART: *Freud had a few things to say, too.*

Freud, the two, the two together. I always consider them as a sort of diabolical pair who were born into our world to destroy it in a very ponderous way. They both wrote so that nobody could read what they wrote, which is a very clever way of doing it because you had to take it on trust.

But as far as the opiates are concerned, I think that television is of course a tremendous opiate. The ordinary citizen today spends statistically about thirty-five hours a week looking in at the television set, which means that he spends twelve years of his three score years and ten engaged in that. A somewhat awesome thought when you consider what the fare provided normally is.

Pascal said that if people cease to believe in God, two possible things happen. One is that they think they are gods themselves and the other is that they revert to pure animality. Therefore they either fall into megalomania or erotomania and those seem to be the two sicknesses of the age and both of them are fantasies which have replaced the great sublime reality of the Christian faith.

There was a novel question in December 1977: 'What is necessary that we may die with dignity?'

What is necessary to be able to die with dignity is to have a faith which projects your existence beyond this present world; to believe, in other words, in God and in man's relationships with God so that, as your life approaches its end, you look into eternity, which is the sequel to your life, and in looking into eternity – as I know myself being near the end of my life – you experience a very great joy, a very great illumination because on the one hand, as you depart from this earth, you are particularly, sharply aware of its beauties, of the delight of human relationship, of the joys of human work, and at the same time you see in the distance what St Augustine called the City of God – you see it quite clearly in the distance – and, in the assurance that your citizenship lies there, the prospect of ending your days in this world is far from being in any way tragic or undignified – becomes no more than like a butterfly shaking itself free of its chrysalis and flying into the sky.

People who are conscious that their life span is over – you can have that consciousness either through being old or you can have it in other ways, through having some incurable disease – for them, leaving this world is enormously helped by being surrounded by loving care, and that is the sort of thing, for instance, Mother Theresa does in Calcutta. She brings in – what in terms of our utilitarian medicine or welfare notions is a perfectly crazy thing – she brings in from the streets people who are dying in order that they may have perhaps just five minutes in the presence of a loving Christian face, and she considers, and I agree with her, that this is infinitely worthwhile, that they should leave this world with an image of love and not with a sense of – alas, as so many human beings have when they come to the end of their days – of simply being rejected, of being unneeded, of being derelict.

That of course is part of it, but the essential thing is to be aware that our time in this world is not the whole story of our existence. Men must believe this, have believed this, will always believe it in one form or another, and it's obviously true.

In September 1979 the team, which included the Labour MP Eric Heffer, was asked whose voice from the past they would be most interested to hear.

I haven't any doubt at all. I would like to hear the Apostle Paul. With all my heart I would love to hear the beginnings of the Christian faith. As I regard the Christian faith as the most important thing that's happened in the world in the last two thousand years, and that there's been a civilisation based upon it – now admittedly coming to an end – I would love to hear the founder of that faith as he first preached the word in the Roman Empire.

HEFFER: *It's not actually the Apostle Paul I would like to hear, although I think I would like to hear him, but I would like to have heard Christ himself. He was actually a bit of a revolutionary in his day. He wanted to change society and I would love to hear exactly what he said.*

Could I explain one thing to Eric? Why did I choose Saint Paul rather than the founder of the Christian religion? Because in a certain humility, I couldn't dare to evoke that voice. But you, as so many people of the Left do, try to present him, as it were, as the Honourable Member for Galilee South!

On Good Friday 1981 a questioner asked: 'As we are commemorating a most important day in the Christian calendar, does the panel feel that a Christian revival is imminent, which will overpower our materialistic society and make for a more caring one?'

I can't say that I feel that a Christian revival is necessarily imminent, but I do detect, in so far as I am able to generalise about such matters, a very great and growing scepticism about the power of a materialist view of life to provide a prosperous and brotherly society; in other words, a considerable scepticism about the sort of Utopias that have been presented since the end of the First World War.

That's a negative point, but of course it does mean that the positive side of this is more open. And as I believe myself, very emphatically, that for Western European people like ourselves, the only valid alternative at the present moment to a materialist view of life is the Christian view of life, therefore I would say that the circumstances are propitious for such a development. And I do note one thing, which in my opinion is the most important thing going on in the world and which, probably for that very reason, is practically never mentioned in the media, that you have this extraordinary fact in our time, that in the part of the world where you would perhaps least expect it, namely in the Soviet Union – which is the first overtly and doctrinally materialistic, atheistic State that has ever existed – in that country and in the most unlikely places in that country, namely the labour camps, you do have the most extraordinary recrudescence of Christian faith. This is an amazing fact which, as a person who has worked as a journalist in the USSR, I would never have anticipated could be possible. But it is happening. And I think it has a very interesting application to the situation in the Western world: that materialism is proving inadequate materially, barren emotionally, and disastrous ethically and spiritually.

THREE

Television

In June 1968 Malcolm wrote in an article that our rulers were fantasy figures in a television Western, and in the following week's programme was invited to comment.

I said that as a result of our mass communication media, notably television, the whole of life was becoming a sort of fantasy, and into that fantasy it was necessary for our rulers to fit. What I was thinking of specifically was the start of all the tele-politics when Nixon and Kennedy were standing against each other and Nixon lost the election because he had this afternoon shadow, and in the Westerns, in which Americans and practically the whole of mankind look for such ideas and values as they have, which isn't saying much, in the Westerns the bad guy always has afternoon shadow and the good guy is properly shaved, and therefore Nixon, by not shaving that day, deprived himself of the Presidency of the United States.

Let me put the same point in a slightly more macabre way. Three weeks ago my eye happened to glance over the TAM [Television Audience Measurement] ratings, and I saw that two shows had tied for ninth place. One was *The Saint* and the other was the murder of Robert Kennedy. In the minds of the people who draw up the TAM ratings, and in the minds of those who seized upon this medium, those two things in a sense are equated. That is what I'm talking about. Our leaders are forced to adjust to that fantasy world.

Malcolm returned to the theme of television's role *vis-à-vis* the American Presidency in August 1973. A questioner had asked whether too much publicity had been given to the Watergate affair. The team also included the writer, Lord Willis.

It has long been my opinion that the unrestrained use of television ultimately makes government impossible and I think that the Watergate affair is illustrating this in a very dramatic way. The point is, you could have done this same thing with any past presidents of my time. I worked as a correspondent in Washington. Certainly, if you'd really done a job on President Truman's entourage in the White House, you could have produced some majestic results. Similarly, if Congress had decided to do a job on President Kennedy at the time of the Bay of Pigs affair, they could have produced the most wonderful television spectacular about false information given.

I'm not concerned to say whether it's good or bad. What I am concerned to say is that it renders government impossible, because if you're going to translate the business of government into a sort of television Western, with a good guy and a bad guy, and you're going to keep that going and produce a big vested interest in keeping it going –

WILLIS: *If you make corrupt government impossible, isn't that a good thing?*

The point that I think perhaps you miss is that all government in a sense is corrupt, that men having power over other men is a corrupt but necessary process. Now, you have done this with Nixon, who is obviously a rather tenth-rate little man ... well, you clap at that, but it's true of a great many rulers, particularly, curiously enough, with universal suffrage democracies, where you tend to elect rather tenth-rate little men. But what this does is that it translates government into a show, and the point is that in this business of exercising authority over other people, you will never have a situation in which you couldn't, if you really wanted to, produce this sort of a show in which people in authority will appear in a very bad light.

I, as a journalist, have been watching governments for the last forty years, and I can't think of any situation in which you couldn't have done this. This is the danger that lies in it.

WILLIS: *You are talking only of America.*

No, I am talking of any country in which I've worked as a journalist, because government itself is a process which, if you translate it into this sort of a spectacular, produces the bad guy and the good guy.

A question about the American Presidential election in May 1980 again enabled Malcolm to return to the theme. The members of the team were asked if they thought the United States was impoverished as far as candidates for the presidency were concerned, and did this pose any danger for the West?

I think this is something that's happening everywhere in the countries that allegedly have democracy, and I think it's to do with television. There are two hundred million Americans; some of them are very clever, intelligent, able. Probably Carter and Reagan represent about the worst you could possibly do. I didn't think very much of Mrs Thatcher or

Callaghan myself. I don't think anything of Giscard. The point is, the sort of leader that comes up out of universal suffrage democracy with television is rather a poor fish. Now, why? I think the reason is this: that what television does to people is it shows them celebrities and so on in terms of what they feel *they* could be. Therefore they want their leaders to give that impression, and nobody could possibly look at Carter and think it's difficult to become President of the United States because obviously it's very easy; and similarly, I think, with Reagan, and similarly with all sorts of people. The idea that you want to be ruled by exceptional people – television kills that. Just as you might say, 'Why is, say, David Frost important?' Well, he's a good enough chap, but I wouldn't have said he had any particular gifts, except this, that when people see him performing on television, they feel – and they're quite right – 'I could do it.' And that is why you are fated, with television, to be ruled by rather tenth-rate people.

Take a simple thing. The President of the United States has to be made up – he's got a make-up man in the White House, and he has to be made up early in the morning in case the cameras should come in. The whole of his life is geared to this public appearance, and I think that is inimical to producing efficient and inspiring people in positions of authority.

Not only that, but as the rather squalid affair of Watergate proved – and I think it was squalid not only in relation to Nixon but also in relation to the people who incessantly went on with it – you had to be prepared for every single bit of your life to be endlessly explored and presented and exaggerated and so on and so on. The point is that only very few people are prepared to face that. You are presenting them with power on terms which would be extremely abhorrent to the most suitable people for exercising power.

When I was working as a correspondent in Washington, we went through all the presidents of the United States and decided which of them would have been the most effective in the age of television, and we decided that it was Warren Harding, the man who poisoned his wife and fortunately died before being found out. The man whose father said to him once, 'Warren, it's a lucky thing that you weren't a girl,' and he said, 'Why?' and his father said, 'Because you'd always be in the family way, you can't say no.' He would have been a splendid television President, and I think that that is where the Western world – and I mean this very seriously – is stepping into disaster, because it has translated authority into terms of public appearance.

Take the case, for instance, of Lord Home, who is a very estimable man. He was completely hopeless as Prime Minister because he looked so funny on television. One of the make-up girls in the BBC said to me, 'Poor Lord Home, he won't ever be any good as Prime Minister because his skin is too tight for his skull.' Do you know, that girl said something true.

I've worked a lot in television – so have you, David [*Jacobs*] – and you know quite well that the people who are most effective in television would by no means be acceptable as the best prime ministers.

Malcolm was always a controversial figure for his views on the Monarchy but, oddly enough, he was seldom required to discuss the subject on the programme. However, there was an exception in June 1969 when a questioner asked whether the image of the Monarchy was enhanced by their appearance on TV.

Whether it is good or bad for the Monarchy is in a way an academic point because it's inescapable. Everything has to go on television and whether that demeans or enhances people, I think it's terribly difficult to say. I mean, the President of the

United States has become a television figure. The Prime Minister has become a television figure. The Leader of the Opposition has become a television figure.

As a person myself – probably the minority of one here – having certain republican predilections, not very keen on monarchies, I would have thought it was likely to protract it rather than to diminish its days, because people will come to see it as something like *Coronation Street* at a very high level. I got into terrible trouble ages ago for writing an article called 'Royal Soap Opera' which was about the Monarchy, in which I said that this was what it had to be in an age of mass communication. And, of course, this *is* in fact what it has got to be and what it is.

On 21 March 1977 a controversial edition of *Panorama* featured a study of a comprehensive school in London, and two weeks later the members of the team were asked what their reaction would be if they had a child going to that school. None of the team had seen the programme, but Malcolm had the best excuse.

I've had my aerials removed and I feel much better for it. They were very neatly removed – it's a kind of mild equivalent of having a prostate operation. Anyway, I read a great deal about this programme, including a long letter from the female who produced it. She said that, despite the cameras, the children behaved perfectly normally. Now, this is utterly ridiculous. One of the great difficulties about all this sort of filming is that no human being ever does behave normally in front of a camera. You imagine telling some children in a class, so they know that it's being filmed – could anybody possibly suppose that the children would then behave normally?

All this idea which is constantly being commended in the *Radio Times* as 'a real-life documentary' is completely bogus. You cannot have real life going on in front of a camera. This is a very important point in connection with the tremendous influence that this sort of documentary has. From what I've heard of that school and from what I've read about that film, I should think in some ways it's probably an understatement, but that's neither here nor there. The public accept it as an authentic picture and by the nature of the case it cannot be an authentic picture. You give me a camera crew and I'll go into any school and I'll produce on the one hand the picture which shows that school as the most idyllic place with this perfect relationship between the staff and the children. Or I'll go into that school with a camera crew and show it as an absolute hotbed of indiscipline and bad language and so on. You can do it all, and if only you could cure people of believing that what the camera shows must be true, it would go a long way towards repairing some of the worst features of our society.

David Jacobs reminded Malcolm of his well-known television interview with Mother Theresa of Calcutta – wasn't she unaware of the camera?

She was a unique case, and you can't argue for a unique case. She was totally unaware of the camera, she'd never heard of cameras, she'd never had anything to do with cameras and therefore she just behaved, thank God, exactly as she normally behaved. But you could never get that with, for instance, a class in a school or just ordinary people, because they are conscious of a camera. Everybody who's worked in this medium knows this. You take a camera in, and immediately you start talking to people they're not really talking to you as they would talk normally, they're talking to the camera.

It's the most terrible thing that's been inflicted on our society, the idea that the camera brings truth. It invariably brings falsity. You can't film truth even if you want to. All those pictures in Vietnam, GIs setting fire to a hut – does anybody suppose that they would be doing that exactly when the camera was perfectly set with the right lighting and everything else? The chances are about ten billion to one. All those things in some degree have to be set up and they are accepted, and increasingly accepted, as being real.

You see a thing in the *Radio Times* – 'a picture of life as it's really lived in China'. Goodness me, if you've ever been to China as a journalist, it's absolutely fantastic – in the first place, you can't see anything unless you're allowed to and it's set up for you to see it. This is the most gigantic fraud that's ever been perpetrated on the public, infinitely worse than the most superstitious superstition in the propagation of religion.

Malcolm returned to the attack on the nature of television in February 1982 when the members of the team, which also included John Mortimer, were asked if they thought that the recent media coverage of riots in several British cities actually increased the likelihood of their happening.

I speak as someone who has been connected, one way and another, with news for the last fifty years in all sorts of capacities – as a reporter, on television, on radio, in newspapers, in magazines. And I say this in complete seriousness – that television, as it becomes increasingly the main source of news, however much the people putting it out may want it not to, will in fact dramatise and falsify the news. It is built into the medium itself.

If you go out with a camera and there's some rioting on, you want to take a picture which will get on the screen in the news broadcast. So you look for things that are happening

which will assist you in getting on to that. And if necessary –
and there's a great deal of evidence of this in connection with
the Vietnam war, when the United States was defeated on the
television screen rather than in the field of battle – you will set
up situations comparable to what you think should be
happening in order to dramatise it further.

Now, this is the trouble. And it's not people sitting in
television set-ups thinking, 'How can I deceive society?' It's
not that at all. They want to make their newscasts effective,
they want to make them striking, they want to get a big
impact from them for every sort of reason. And in doing that,
with the apparatus at their disposal, they will in fact
dramatise the situation and thereby accentuate it.

In some of the American racial riots, the cameras were
removed from the scene and it is a fact that the rioting tended
to subside. This is not because the rioting was due to the
cameras but it is because, in so far as you present the scene
with the camera, you are forced by the nature of the medium
to dramatise it.

Now, this is the most serious circumstance, politically
speaking, in the world today. Of course, in the totalitarian
countries it doesn't arise because the television – like
everything else – conveys just one picture. Nobody's going
wandering round with cameras in Afghanistan at this
moment – that won't happen. But every now and again, some
suitable picture of what's going on in Afghanistan will be
dished up for the Soviet public. But as for we Western
countries that want to leave these means of communication
completely free and untrammelled, we will be at the mercy,
not of the deceitfulness of people operating television, but by
the sheer fantasy of television itself.

I tell you one last point. I could take a camera crew to South
Africa and I could come back with two perfectly valid and
applauded documentaries. And one would show that in South
Africa there is the most amicable and beautiful relationship
between races ever known, and the other would show that

never had there been such horrible hatred stirred up between races as in South Africa. And both would be valid. That is the danger of this medium, and after many years working in it and much thinking about it and writing about it, I say this: that with unimpeded use of television, no country will ever be able to win a war, put down an insurrection and, ultimately, to govern itself.

We who work in television, we know that we have created a sort of Moloch, something that is beyond control. I'm not saying that people are trying to distort facts. John speaks of reporting in words in a newspaper and television as though they were the same thing. But when you read a report, an article in a paper, you know that that is a man's view, an individual's view, even if it's not signed. But when people see the work of the camera, they still think that that is reality. And it's just as remote from reality as the most fanciful type of writing.

This is what I'm trying to say, that we are up against something quite different that's never existed before and we don't know how to cope with it.

FOUR

Medicine and Health

In October 1954 a questioner asked: 'Should there be private beds in hospitals available for paying patients?' Malcolm, as was often his wont, waited until the Members of Parliament, in this case Hugh Gaitskell and Walter Elliot, had had their say.

Nothing could be more fascinating to me than to listen to these two eminent politicians debating this question. I myself have no strong views on it, I simply point out this: that it is one of the basic dilemmas that arise from the present situation of our society. On the one hand, we are telling people that it is absolutely wrong that there should be any inequality, and any honest man must assent to that. On the other hand, we are asking people to save, to provide for their future, to pursue their own interests and ends. Now, these two things are in fact incompatible, and this business of these hospital beds illustrates it well.

If you say to a man – you appeal to him on the wireless – you say, 'You must save in order that you may assure your future, be able to look after your dependents,' that's one thing. On the other hand, you say that if a man benefits in any way from doing that, he's a sort of a criminal because he is going against the temper of an egalitarian society; he's jumping the queue, he's seizing advantages by virtue of the fact that he has accumulated a certain amount of money.

Now what I say to you is – being a complete anarchist, and belonging to neither of these distinguished parties – what I say is that what you cannot do is to have it both ways. You can either say to people, 'By all means save, look after yourselves, try and make your circumstances comfortable,'or say that no one has any right to more than any other person and that society must provide equally for all. Both these are tenable propositions. What is not a tenable proposition is to say that both are applicable at the same time.

In October 1965 a team which also included Baroness Summerskill and Lord Boothby was asked: 'Many people suffer from an incurable disease and a great deal of pain. Should not the medical profession be allowed to end their suffering?' In a recent court case, a man had been found guilty of murdering his son but given two years' probation, as his son had been dying in agony from cancer and Lady Summerskill, herself a qualified doctor, spoke approvingly of the judge: 'He was a wonderful man. He decided that he would not just interpret the letter of the law. He looked at all the circumstances, and in his wisdom and his humanity he recognised that that father had one motive only, and that was to save the suffering of his beloved son.' However, the team was against legislation on euthanasia. Lord Boothby said he was perfectly content to leave it to the judgement and wisdom of the medical profession.

I think this is the most terrible proposition that could possibly be made – that a doctor, merely a professionally qualified person, often a quack and a charlatan, should be entrusted by society with the right to put out a human life. This shocks me profoundly and utterly. On what conceivable basis can he decide whether life should be continued or not?

I go further and I say that the judge who's been quoted with approval here as having said to a man who'd murdered his son, 'You did right' – such a judge should be hounded out of court, because he is holding out to every single person who may grow tired of looking after some unfortunate and hopeless invalid, holding out to them the right to end that life.

Now, I think if you believe, as every Christian must, that a man exists on this earth as part of the Divine Plan ... that a human being should have the arrogance to say, 'I decide *that* life is not worth living, and I on my responsibility put it out' – such a thought would only occur in this base and materialist age in which we are living.

Bob, let's be clear what you said. You said, 'Fortunately, there's no need for legislation in this matter because we can leave it in the hands of doctors and they will, when they so decide, administer excessive drugs so that the patient dies.' If you would seriously say of someone you devoutly loved to a doctor, 'I leave it in your hands to put out this life when you wish to,' very well, but we must recognise that if that is to be accepted as the moral basis of our society, then we have turned our back on the whole tradition of the Christian religion.

Lady Summerskill pointed out that other countries agreed that we had the finest judiciary in the world and she said further words in defence of the judge, who 'in his wisdom decided to temper justice with mercy and allow the father to go unpunished.'

I'm sorry, Lady Summerskill, that isn't the point. He said he committed no wrong. This is what I object to. I don't in the least object to a judge saying, 'I have considered all these circumstances and I believe that mercy is here called for.' He went much further than that. He wouldn't allow the Clerk of the Court – as I read the proceedings – to admit that in fact a crime had been committed. A crime *had* been committed, because to take a life – any life, according to our religion – is a crime. Because what will you have tomorrow? Some other father – whose son is perhaps not quite as bad as this – reads this. 'My boy's suffering. I must stop his suffering.' He quotes the precedent of this judge; and whatever view you may take, Lady Summerskill, of the quality of our judiciary – and I don't share your admiration wholly – whatever view you take, at least it is not a judge's business to say that breaking the law is not wrong. He can say that the law is wrong and the law should be changed. But as the law stands – and in my opinion, rightly stands – that father committed a crime. The judge can ask for mercy but he can't say it's not a crime.

In 1968 there was a great deal of publicity about the successful heart transplant operation carried out in South Africa by Dr Christian Barnard, and in June of that year a questioner asked whether money used on heart and kidney transplants in Great Britain would be better spent on the National Health Service as a whole.

I happen to loath the whole idea of these heart transplant operations. I find them deeply repellent morally – as a lot of people do, as a matter of fact, more than is sometimes recognised. The whole idea of regarding a human being – who I consider to be made in the image of his Creator – as a collection of spare parts which can be used to patch up other collections of spare parts, is to me deeply abhorrent.

I tried to explain this to Dr Christian Barnard and other doctors once on a television programme with a notable lack of success. I found that they really didn't know what I was talking about at all, which only confirmed the idea that doctors are the last people in the world who should be able to decide when people's organs may be removed.

Then, with regard to the question of priorities, of course I agree with the questioner. I think that it's the most monstrous perversion of priorities, and I think that in the history books of our time, one of the most terrible things will be that in the continent of Africa, which lacks even the minimum medical requirements, even just medicines and prophylactics, an enormous apparatus of medicine was set up in order to give, in a tremendous blaze of publicity, a heart transplant to a middle-aged dentist. That that should be the position of the white man in this vast, backward continent, will, I think, be in the history books a most disgraceful item.

Malcom was equally condemnatory later in the year when there was a discussion about the use of the fertility drug.

I have to confess to you that I have the utmost suspicion of the use of these drugs because I think there are tremendous dangers in this interfering too much with the natural processes of human beings and of nature and of everything else. You see, at the moment man is in a particularly arrogant mood and he's interfering with everything, in matters of fertilisers and so on, and I think it's full of the most appalling dangers.

When I read about these six children born through this drug, I said it was utterly squalid and horrible. And so I would adopt the most stringent attitude, if it was in my power to do so, about their use, which amounts in practice to experimenting with human beings. Don't deceive yourselves. In matters of the heart transplant and these drugs and all the things that geneticists are planning, of which this is only a tiny little foretaste, they are experimenting; and I disapprove of experimenting with human beings because I hold human beings in too great respect.

In June 1970 a questioner asked why abortion should be permissible when capital punishment was not. Malcolm ignored the matter of capital punishment and concentrated on abortion.

I would wish to pay public tribute to some nurses that I read about who declined to participate in these loathsome operations. I would like to say how enormously I admire them and agree with them. Actually, the point about abortion is not just simply taking the appalling step of putting out a life which had begun to form itself, but also in accepting the idea that it is permissible for society to step in so that every pregnant woman who happens to be in a mood – which most pregnant women have at some time, as we all know – of not wanting to go on and have the baby, she's free to go and have it removed.

The Act was a vicious Act; its consequences have been shameful and deplorable, and it is my earnest hope that the new House of Commons will set itself before very long scrupulously and strictly to revise it. It's by no means certain that there are fewer back street abortions as a result of this law. In fact, in countries which have completely permissive abortions you very often have more back street abortions; the hospitals are cluttered up with people. Of course it's a bad law.

But I would go further and say that though there are certainly exceptional cases where, with the utmost care and reverence, a birth which is developing should be terminated, I think that any law which makes it possible easily, lightly to terminate a pregnancy is a thoroughly vicious one.

And I'll tell you another thing about it, which you probably won't agree with, but sure as fate, as this law becomes established, it will be followed by another and that will be euthanasia. You will find that this will follow from it – that the nasty, the horrible, anti-Christian idea that there is no reason why we should go to all this trouble to maintain the lives of people who are mentally negligible and senile, that dreadful idea will begin to grow stronger, that we can get rid of them; and we can get rid of them as we love to get rid of things on the basis of a lot of false humanitarianism.

Malcolm returned to this theme in November 1975 when a questioner asked whether there was sufficient caution in releasing patients from mental institutions.

The reality behind it is that there is a terrible shortage of staff for looking after people like this, that we are not producing people who are prepared to do this sort of work. I have a friend who was in Broadmoor; I'm a godfather of his child and he's absolutely OK, I think. But we go to all this talk about should they be let out or should they not, while the fact is that the facilities available for looking after these people are strictly limited and are getting less. And therefore quite often the real reason why they're let out is that there is no means of keeping them. So it's not much good our saying, 'I think they ought to be looked after better and I think this or perhaps that ought to happen,' unless we've got some answer to this question of how in a society like ours you induce people to do these jobs that are very disagreeable and very painful.

I don't think a proper answer to that has been found, and so really the argument in the newspapers about it is not – and in my experience as a journalist this is very, very often the case – not about the thing itself, the real question; it's about a suppositional question that if you did this or that, it would be all right. But you can't do this because you haven't got the people to do it.

I'm going to make a sinister prophecy that nobody will agree with, that if this problem goes on and we go on evading the reality of it, there will come a demand for euthanasia, there will come a demand for solving this problem by liquidating people who represent a difficult problem. And it will be a very black and terrible day when that happens. It's already started, as a matter of fact. I mean this case that's going on in America, this girl who is being kept alive. And the interesting thing is that it's presented as a sort of curtain raiser, a sort of soap opera, with the goodies who are all the people who think the machine should be turned off, and the baddies who are the people who raise the question of whether you are entitled to do it.

FIVE

Race Relations

In February 1968 the team was asked to discuss the Asian immigrants coming into the United Kingdom at that time. Enoch Powell had by then made some of his extensively-reported speeches on immigration.

I say with the utmost frankness that if I were in power I would totally, as far as was possible, totally stop immigrants into this country from Africa, Asia and the West Indies at this time; and I would not lift that until I was completely satisfied that those who are already here were properly, fairly, justly, equitably incorporated in the population.

Now, there's an enormous amount of humbug in this question, and what in fact we pay for in life, collectively and individually, is not so much our viciousness as our humbug. We pretended that the Commonwealth, the old Empire and the Commonwealth, was a multi-racial organisation. It never was. It was a piece of complete humbug. We are now paying for that humbug by being confronted with it in the form of these people coming in; and we all know, every single person in this country knows absolutely, that we are laying up a monstrous, wicked problem for our future people. We know we're doing it, we know that we'll have the same trouble that they've had so gruesomely and horribly in America. How extraordinary that we should voluntarily create it!

Now, when Enoch Powell, for whom I have a very high

respect because he's a truthful man, when he said this the other day, everybody jumped on him – said he's a racialist. He wasn't a racialist. He was trying to prevent racialism poisoning this country.

That's what I'd do if it rested with me but I'm quite sure that our politicians won't do that. They will continue to equivocate and in so doing they will both be cruel to the people coming here, because they'll bring them in when there's no proper life for them, no proper accommodation for them, and cruel to posterity, to our people, who will suddenly be confronted with this trouble in our island, where we never had any trouble of this kind, where we incorporated people of all nationalities, of all races, into this country.

We shall have it; and we shall have it because of this sentimental piece of humbug, because people will not admit that people, quite apart from race, who have a different economic standard cannot live peaceably side by side in the same country.

We in fact derived great wealth from our colonisation in Africa and from our rule in India. Great wealth flowed into our country because of that. Nobody who studies the history of the thing can possibly doubt it. But it would be a ridiculous return for that to welcome into our country people we cannot accommodate, whom we cannot give good lives to, whom we cannot provide proper education for. Far better, if our consciences trouble us, to help them with all sorts of economic aid.

A year later Enoch Powell was suggesting that immigrants who wished to return home should be given £2,000 to assist them, and in June 1969, a questioner asked the team to comment.

I think the payments side of this is rather ludicrous because it is obvious that if you say £2,000 you set up a sort of Dutch auction. Also I think that as most English people can't distinguish between one Pakistani or Indian and another, what they'd do would be to collect their two thousand, go out, smuggle their way in and then come as another.

But I would like to make one point about this: I don't think the idea of facilitating people leaving the country if they genuinely want to leave it is itself a racist idea. I think this is absolute nonsense. I'll tell you a curious thing that I happened to come across the other day, that Abraham Lincoln, at one point when he was struggling with the slavery question in the United States before the Union, actually considered the idea of repatriating all the American Negroes back to Africa. Now, does that make Abraham Lincoln a racist? Of course not. He was simply considering a problem that had arisen. He saw looming ahead exactly what happened in the United States and he toyed with this idea. No doubt he found it to be impractical.

Now, I think it is the most preposterous nonsense to suggest that it is racist to explore the possibility that people who come and settle in this country might want to go back and if they want to go back they should be helped to go back – there is nothing racist about this at all. Of course if it was to be compulsory or something like that, it would be quite different. That should be put out of your mind. But the idea of putting down £2,000 and bartering in that sort of way would turn out to be totally impractical and I think Mr Powell is weak on finance.

I don't think my worst enemy could call me a racist. I have

the honour of having been barred from entering the Union of South Africa – that's my credential. Now, if I'd said that in my opinion, like Mr Powell, I see that the presence of coloured people in this country in the present circumstances may lead to serious trouble if some of those people are unhappy and uncomfortable here and want to return to their countries, it would be the height of folly not, in the most humane and decent way, to enable them to do so; if I say that, I am not being a racist.

Enoch Powell was himself on the team when in June 1976 there was a question about assimilating immigrants.

It's perfectly true that this country has excelled in assimilating people, but there are two things to be considered about the special case at issue which is different from any previous case.

The first is the numbers of people. They're very greatly in excess of any numbers that have ever had to be assimilated before. Secondly – which is always forgotten in this discussion but it's very important – do they in fact wish to be assimilated? And I think you will find that one of the many difficulties of this particular situation is that many of the immigrants from Asia and from Africa and the West Indies do not in fact wish to be assimilated. They maintain their separateness, and that is why I don't think you can equate the situation that confronts us now with the situation that confronted us when, for instance, you had a lot of German Social Democrats coming here or when you had a lot of fugitives from this or that monarchy or revolution. That is a different thing; and I think it is quite a serious problem.

I think it is the most reprehensible and monstrous thing that people who express anxiety about this situation should be condemned and blackguarded as racialists. It is a legitimate source of anxiety to every sort of British citizen. And what we haven't mentioned and what has a great deal to do with this anxiety is that, first of all, we've found that a great many of the statistics that are given are in fact fraudulent or wrong; and secondly, that this is a sort of indefinite obligation, this is not a thing where you can say, 'Well, now it's gone, now we've settled it. We'll accept X thousand more and then it's finished.' It appears to be an unending responsibility and that, I think, is what is people's anxiety.

Now, if you create the feeling that to express this anxiety in any way is to be a fascist or a blackguard, then you will be doing the best you can to promote serious racial trouble, because people will bottle this up because they will be afraid or ashamed to express it and then when the explosion comes, if it does, it will to that extent be worse. If the Government, or any government in power, wishes to make a serious contribution to what is growing into a very, very ugly situation, there's one thing they can do: let the British public know the extent of the commitment. Let them define it. Let them tell us what we are really committed to, what is the limit, if any, because I think the English people are entitled to know that.

Huge figures are flourished about. It's said that if, for instance, trouble arose in Malaya there could be a million or more Malays who could claim British passports and the right to come here. We ought to know whether these things are facts or not; otherwise, with this question driven to some extent down into our subconscious because of the rather fatuous attempt to legislate about people's attitudes – which is always a great mistake – people may be conceiving nightmares which are quite wrong; but they ought to be given the actual commitment, what it is we are committed to.

The riots in Brixton in April 1981 seemed to some people to justify the forebodings Enoch Powell had first voiced some fourteen years earlier. The following week the members of the team were asked what they considered to be the root causes of the riots and how they would prevent similar incidents happening again.

It seems to me that the Commissioner of the Metropolitan Police, David McNee, had a very good point when he said that it was difficult to believe that the thing happened spontaneously as a result of this single incident, when there was a whole supply of petrol bombs to hand. I think that's a very valid point.

With regard to the question of unemployment, supposing that this so-called economic depression which we're now apparently suffering passes, it's very questionable to me whether you would find that there were jobs available for these young coloured people in Brixton. You know, it will be very strange and ironical in the history books. They'll say, here we were with this very large and growing problem of unemployment, and at the same time, of course, compared with the depression of the Thirties – I was a young journalist in Manchester at the time of that depression and saw quite a lot of it. People say, 'Wasn't it roughly the same?' No, it wasn't. And the three factors that were different were: first of all, that we didn't then have a largish alien population living among us who all required jobs; secondly, we didn't encourage by every means possible the employment of women in jobs, other than being at home; and finally, we didn't have this increasing development of technology which, of course, all the time is creating unemployment. So that you've got three things going on, calculated to create unemployment, quite irrespective of this economic depression.

And I think there's a good deal of rather childish feeling

that after all the depression will pass and then magically all these young black people will have employment. I don't think they will. I think we've got to go deeper into the question than that, and decide what we're really going to do about having a lot of young kids who are rather poorly educated on the whole – perhaps no fault of theirs – haven't a great deal to offer in the way of employment. How are we really going to cope with that?

What happened in America is, of course, very interesting. One thing that happened was that in certain cases, where there had been racial rioting somewhat like what happened in Brixton, the media, the television cameras, were cleared out and there was no television, and it is clear that the trouble abated. In other words, to a certain extent, and I'm sure this is true, the presence of cameras stirs up the trouble, partly because there is this terrible element of exhibitionism in everybody so that when they know they're going to be filmed, they'll go to very great lengths, even to the extent of murdering John Lennon or having a shot at the President of the United States, in order to do it. That figures in it.

But I think you have to be careful about equating the American situation with the situation here, because the American economy could absorb the black employees. But what I question – I'd be very interested to know what the answer to it is – is can our economy absorb all the people who are unemployed or who are likely to be unemployed, given that they all expect a job, and that all women should be entitled, if they wish to, to take jobs, and that technology should go on being developed, each new development of which involves a great number of people losing their jobs? Those are the three factors that I see contributing to make me very doubtful whether in the best possible circumstances the actual employment situation will be enormously better.

SIX

Russia and Communism

In March 1952 a questioner asked: 'In view of the political, financial and economic chaos and instability caused by the armaments race, does it not appear to the team that Russia is winning the battle of Europe more surely and more effectively than by attempting to destroy it with atom bombs?'

First of all, the armaments race is a thing that cuts both ways. In so far as Russia imposes the armaments race on the world, she also has to arm herself and therefore whatever economic weakening results from spending an undue proportion of national wealth on armaments affects Russia just as much as the Western world.

Secondly, I would say that even if it were the case that re-arming was producing excessive economic disequilibrium, there would be circumstances in which it was necessary to undertake it; and in order to make that point I would ask you to cast your minds back to the years before the 1939–45 War. Precisely the same arguments would have applied in regard to re-arming against the Nazis. There were many then who advocated not re-arming and their voices unfortunately were heeded, with the result that when 1939 came along the catastrophe was infinitely greater than it might have been – in fact, it might have been avoided altogether.

Therefore I don't see that you can look at a question like re-arming solely in terms of its economic consequence. You have to decide what degree of re-armament is necessary in order to achieve some sort of national or Western security and having decided that, you have to do it, and if you are going to go on existing as a country you have to undertake that burden and make the requisite sacrifice. The only possible alternative to that is simply surrendering and saying, 'We can't do this and therefore we cease to be a factor in world politics.'

In 1955 the leaders of the Soviet Union, Bulganin and Khrushchev, made disparaging remarks about Great Britain while they were on a visit to India. In December of that year a questioner asked whether, in view of these remarks, their visit to this country should be cancelled.

I think that if you invite two people officially to come and visit your country, you imply a certain attitude towards them. And I think that the unspeakable lies and ill manners of these two characters in India and Burma are such that it would reflect very ill upon the British Government that they should be invited here.

I apply exactly the same standards to an official invitation here as I would to a personal invitation, and had I invited someone to dinner and found that they had publicly committed themselves to the opinion that I was a very offensive person, that my behaviour had been corrupt and evil in the past, I would be very inclined to send a rather cold note saying that after all the dinner party was off. And I think it would be highly desirable that the British Government should express its repugnance and distaste for the remarks that have been made by these two people in an area of the world which still passes for being part of the British Commonwealth, by cancelling the invitation that's been given them to come here.

I also think of the many refugees living in this country for whom it is an utter insult that, after what's been said about us and about what we've done in the past, they should come here as the official guests of the British Government and the British Crown.

There seems to me a very close parallel between this question and one that I've just been reading about in the life of Geoffrey Dawson, the late Editor of *The Times*. There was the question of getting Goering over to London – could Goering be persuaded to come to London and see the Grand National? Now, at that time I strongly felt – as, I'm happy to say, did a great many people in England – that in view of the loathsome and offensive things that Goering was constantly saying, it was highly undesirable that he should come as a public guest of the British Government.

Realistic conversations are always desirable but I do not think that the way to achieve those realistic conversations is to pretend that you can invite and entertain and consort with people such as Goering or Bulganin or Khrushchev, whose public attitude is ceaselessly and constantly insulting to everything that you represent.

A year later, after the Suez crisis and the concurrent Russian invasion of Hungary, the team was asked if a third world war was inevitable.

History shows that nothing is inevitable, ever has been, ever could be. If there is to be a third world war we will not in fact be a principal in it. In other words, the decision as to whether that war is to take place at all will not be a decision that we take; and that is in a way rather pleasant and enables one, as one grows older, to grow more frivolous and lighthearted, because the agony of history before the 1939–45 War was the feeling that our decision was a vital one. Now we're not in that position at all and if this third world war is going to happen, it won't be by any decision that we've taken. In fact, I think it would be a terribly good thing for us to get right into our heads the idea that what we think about it is not of major importance.

Obviously nobody wants a third world war and when these two estimable Members of Parliament [*David Price and Dr Dickson Mabon*] talk about convincing the Russian people that a third world war is undesirable – there is no means of convincing the Russian people of anything, because that is a dictatorial government. Nor is there any possibility of making any sort of deals with dictatorial governments – but I should have said that for the first time there was a real hope as a result of these incidents in Hungary, which I think are the most hopeful things that have happened in the world since the end of the 1939–45 War because what that has shown is that fourteen armoured divisions can't hold down an utterly unarmed, hungry people who want to be free.

In December 1957 the team was asked whether there was a possibility of Communism gaining control of Great Britain. Malcolm's article about the Royal Family, 'Royal Soap Opera', had recently been published in America.

I think that the defence against Communism is to safeguard freedom – freedom in all its senses. And having been bashed about a bit recently for having expressed views which were not enormously popular, I feel this more strongly than ever. It is absolutely true that you can only stand up against the threat of totalitarian tyranny by securing and ensuring your own freedom and to the extent that the English were ever to become conformists, were ever to accept mass hysteria as distinct from independent thought, the danger of Communism would be to that extent greater.

In November 1968 the programme visited the Royal Naval College at Dartmouth. One of the cadets referred to the increasing Russian naval presence in the Mediterranean and asked what NATO should do about it.

Either there's a world war about the Mediterranean and the Middle East or there isn't. If there's a world war about the Mediterranean and the Middle East, then everything and everyone is involved. If there isn't, I can't see that the fact that this Russian fleet is steaming about in the Mediterranean matters any more than any other ship steaming about in the Mediterranean.

I can't help suspecting that we think in terms of situations which have ceased to be relevant. It's like when the Suez trouble was on and everybody said, 'Once we lose the Suez Canal, we've lost the lifeline of our something-or-other.' And a man sitting at the dinner table moves the cruet over like that and says, 'There's the Gulf of Aqaba.' Then they move up the spoons like that, saying, 'You get a force coming in there.' I suspect that all this is a lot of complete baloney. We haven't had the Suez Canal for months and all that's happened is that Mr Onassis has got richer.

In August 1975 a team which included Lord Hailsham was asked a question about the Helsinki Agreement with the Soviet Union on the subject of human rights.

The thing that astonishes me about this Helsinki business is that anybody on earth should attach the slightest importance to it. I mean, the various undertakings that were given have all been given twenty or thirty times before in various instruments and agreements which have not had the slightest effect. Why anybody should think that now they will is beyond my comprehension.

I read in *The Times* this morning, in a letter from a Member of Parliament, that the Prime Minister, Harold Wilson, had stated that if the Helsinki Agreement had been made at the time, the Russians would never have occupied Czechoslovakia. Honestly, I can only say that to feel that our affairs are in the hands of a man who can take that view extinguishes whatever faint glimmer of hope for the future that I might have.

Do you think that any single thing agreed at Helsinki – that there's the faintest chance of its being observed? The Russians have promised to allow free entry and exit into their country. Do you see the faintest reason to suppose it's going to happen? The Helsinki Agreement is just a nonsense. What advantage accrues to us – and honestly, I ask this for information – what advantage accrues to us in making agreements which are broken before we make them, and which there's not the faintest, smallest chance will ever be observed?

HAILSHAM: *We have to live with the Communist world, divided between Russia and China. If we refuse to talk to them, if we refuse to find some points upon which at least we can make them make undertakings, whether they keep them or not, I think the result will be bad for us and bad for the things we believe in. It was I who, on behalf of this country, negotiated the partial test ban agreement. It has, by and large, been kept by the Russians. It has been kept by the Americans. It's been kept by this country. It did good. I had no illusions about the Russians, or for that matter about the Americans, when I negotiated it, but I'm not at all ashamed of having done so.*

Why should you be ashamed? You simply don't understand the point that's being made. The point that's being made is not that we should separate ourselves from the Russians, stand aloof from the Russians. I ask, as a simple journalist, what is the point of entering into an agreement that is broken before you begin it and cannot possibly be observed? These agreements have been made ever since the covenant of the United Nations was agreed. They have been made over and over again, and never kept. Now you say there is some extraordinary advantage in making that agreement yet again.

SEVEN

Education

In March 1957 a team which included Jack Longland, the Director of Education for Derbyshire, was asked: 'It is claimed that all children of sufficiently high intelligence can receive a free academic education; should parents therefore make great sacrifices to send their children to a public school?'

As far as the first part of the question is concerned, you can't make a generalisation like that, but there has been an enormous move in the direction of children of sufficiently high intelligence being able to receive a free academic education.

Now, with regard to the second part, I find myself in a minority because I think that the reason that people send children to these public schools is not at all because they think it's a better education – Jack Longland said it's not a better education – they send them there, if we're going to call a spade a spade, for purely snobbish reasons. They send them there because they think these schools will turn out a product who, in his clothes, manner of speech and general behaviour, will seem to be upper class, or *U*.

Now, is it desirable that a society like ours, given the various trends that we notice in it, should consist of two different types of persons? I most emphatically say, no. I think that it's a very undesirable thing that there should be a minority of boys who have been to schools which are calculated to turn them out as being different from all the rest, especially as, with the political pressures that exist, the economic advantages of that difference are doing to dwindle more and more and more and it's going to become a pure Mitfordian fatuity.

So far as I'm concerned, I think that the parents who make sacrifices to send a child to a public school are rather in the same position as my favourite character in fiction, Don Quixote. He made great sacrifices to equip himself with that armour, to purchase that poor old bony horse called Rocinante, and he went riding away on his horse, but it was a completely foolish undertaking, foolish because it bore no relationship to the society in which Don Quixote was living.

Malcolm returned to the attack on public schools in October 1961. In a question arising out of a debate on education at the Labour Party Conference, the members of the team were asked for their views on the party's aim to turn public schools from playing grounds for plutocrats into training grounds for democrats.

The point is, what sort of society is going to come to pass in the twentieth century? Now, if that sort of society requires using every single resource of intelligence and ability, then this very specialised type of education which, whatever you may say, produces people who feel themselves to be different and perhaps a cut above products of other schools, is going to be a heavy disadvantage, an economic and social disadvantage.

Now, the pleasure of countries like America and Canada and Australia and, may I say it, even Scotland, where this question doesn't arise, is that when a man is applying for a job, the last thing in the world anybody thinks is, 'What school was he at?' The question doesn't arise because they know that he was at the school that everybody else went to.

Now, in my opinion – and I might be wrong, but this is my opinion – the sort of society that we have got to develop in order to hold our own in the twentieth century is a society in which one man and another starts off from scratch in the struggle to earn a living and to exert his abilities; and that won't come as long as you allow people to spend these increasing sums of money, which often cripple them, in order to have an education and – don't cheat yourselves – they don't pay that money because it's a better education – in most cases it's not better. They pay it for snobbish reasons. They pay it in order that their son or daughter should emerge from it as having a snob status. That's what the money's paid for, and I'm against it.

In May 1968, at a time of considerable student unrest both in Great Britain and in France, the team was asked: 'How is it that, although opportunities for further education in this country are today greater than ever before, students are demonstrating against college authorities more than ever before, although the latter are more permissive than ever before?'

To a great extent what these young people are suffering from in my experience is conceit, because there's such an enormous amount of flattery. They're subjected to flattery as part of this very morbid cult of youth, and also from advertisers and people like that. Now, that is very bad for the old but I think it might be even worse for the young.

Another point is that the actual standards of university education are steadily falling, particularly in these bogus subjects, these bogus schools, sociology and things like that, with the result that these students are really not, in the proper sense of the word, educated at all.

We try to persuade ourselves that there are specific causes for their unrest. We say, 'Well, there were two world wars,' or we say, 'The society that they're being asked to be members of isn't a suitable one,' and so on. I think this is largely baloney, that in fact they are simply young yahoos.

The truth is that you cannot have order in a society at any level unless you have some sort of moral order. Social order, political order, any kind of order, is a consequence of moral order. There is no moral order, particularly among these young people, and therefore there can be no social or political order. They are not, in fact, agitating for particular things. They're just disruptive.

Now, the big joke to me in this whole student business was when I read, to my great delight, that the students in Sweden had revolted. I thought this was the height of comedy, because of all the things that are said about students – Sweden was not in the war, Sweden's not an atomic power, Sweden does not approve of Vietnam, Sweden hands out contraceptives with the morning tea – all the sort of thing they're supposed to be revolting about is available in Sweden.

Malcolm's disenchantment with higher education was further displayed in November of that year when a questioner asked: 'There has been increased spending on higher education but a cut-back in spending on nursery education; have we got our priorities right?' The team also included the

Bishop of Crediton and Bamber Gascoigne, the chairman of *University Challenge*.

I can see the implication of this question is that we ought to spend less on higher education and more on primary education, and I entirely agree. Judging by the public behaviour of people who are receiving higher education, I would be very pleased to see a lot of institutions for higher education shut down completely. And instead of squandering grants on completely worthless individuals who have no particular desire to study, I would like to take all that away and improve enormously the quality of teaching, the pay of teachers in primary schools.

Bamber assumes – everybody always does on this programme – that we all think that the more money you spend on education the better. I don't think this at all. I think that an enormous amount of money is absolutely wasted on education.

The Bishop said we had extended higher education in order to make ourselves more efficient; but have we made ourselves more efficient? As far as I can understand, the most popular school at these universities today is sociology, and no one has ever been able to tell me any useful thing that a sociologist can do of any sort of description.

By 1972 Malcolm's views on universities had undergone no change whatsoever. In March of that year the team was asked whether young people at universities were making the most of their opportunities; but that did not discourage Malcolm from discussing the question which had been asked three and a half years earlier.

I think these universities have become totally farcical

institutions and I should very much like to see them shut down for a year or two in order to begin again and think it over. Particularly that's true, I think, of the sociological departments. I would like to see it all shut down, give everybody time to think a little and then perhaps, rather prudently and carefully, open them up again. But I would say that as of now they are a total waste of public money. I think that the great expansion of universities has taken place without any real thought as to what their purpose is, what they're trying to do, and that in many cases they are producing people who don't get jobs because in fact they're not particularly useful at anything in particular. In other words, they're following an idea that more higher education is *per se* good. A great many institutions have been expanded without any clear idea as to how or why they're being expanded, and without adequate staff or foresight in setting them up, and the result is that you are over-producing a certain type of graduate, wasting resources which would be far better spent on improving the lower levels of education which are sorely in need of money.

Seven months later the Queen visited Stirling University and there was a great deal of publicity about the somewhat loutish behaviour of some of the students towards her. A question on this gave Malcolm an opportunity to recall his 'Royal Soap Opera' article.

This question has a special interest for me because I got into terrific trouble a number of years ago for writing an article which was considered to be very critical of the Monarchy, and indeed it did criticise the manner in which it was being conducted at that time and certain aspects of what I considered to be excessive adulation. Well, things have changed a good deal since then.

I knew this question would come up, of course, and one's natural impulse is to say 'Abominable behaviour' and I think it *was* abominable behaviour in so far as we've received a correct account of it. I think what was abominable about it, in so far as we can judge, was simply using an occasion in which someone is invited to a university to be insulting. This has happened to me, as a matter of fact, in visiting a university, and it's a very disconcerting thing. I agree that the Queen behaved with great calm, much more so than I did in a similar case.

It's a sad business that one should have this sort of atmosphere at a university, and there's something gone mad about this idea of setting up university after university and having a type of education – which is very dubious at the best – of universal application. It's something that ought to be thought out, because it would be a sad thing if it came to be true – and I've sometimes thought it might – that we might be the first civilisation in history that didn't go down because we were invaded by barbarians, but because we produced our own barbarians at the public expense in the course of reading for university degrees.

In January 1976 the team was invited to comment on a proposal by the Education Officer of the Alcohol Advisory Centre that young people should be encouraged to drink moderately at home in order to take the myth out of alcohol.

This proposal supports a conviction I've long had that the whole educational system in this country is in the hands of lunatics. There is no other possible explanation. Everybody

knows the most alarming and horrible and disgusting thing –
that alcoholism is on the increase among school children. This
is a shameful and horrible fact.

The story goes on in the paper even better than the
question. The man says, and I think it's awfully nice of him,
he says, 'I wouldn't actually oblige parents who are total
abstainers to offer drink to their children, I wouldn't oblige
them to.' We who are total abstainers thank this gentleman
who thinks we may not actually have to give our children or
our grandchildren drinks, which is terribly nice of him, very
considerate.

My dear friends, this is going on in our country, this kind of
utter lunacy in which you're confronted with something like
taking marijuana and they say, 'Well, let's smoke pot at home
all together with the tiny tots coming in, let's hand out birth
pills to the Brownies, let's have sex education in our play
schools, and then we'll get better and more serene.' And every
one of these things that's done, this horrible situation of
children being drunkards and precocious, and girls of eleven
having abortions, is done more and more and more.

You know, I've got a nightmare which afflicts me every
time I come on this programme, and that is that I'm sitting in
an underground BBC studio and up aloft the mushroom
clouds are forming and the last vestige of what's called
civilisation is coming to an end, and somebody says, 'What do
the panel think about the growth of juvenile delinquency?'
Everybody says, 'Well, I think we need more sex education in
our schools.' That's my nightmare.

On a visit to Northern Ireland in May 1980 the members of
the team were asked whether they thought integrated

education could make a major contribution to the healing of sectarian divisions in the Province.

I think this idea that you can do such wonderful things with education is pretty beside the point. All my life, and I am seventy-seven years old, I've been hearing people say, 'With more and better education, everything's going to get better.' What happened has been that more and more is spent on education, illiteracy has increased and every type of misbehaviour has multiplied in the schools, and I'm not sure that it wouldn't happen here.

I was very taken the other day by some embittered schoolmaster who was asked to give a definition of education, and he gave what I thought was a very brilliant one. He said, 'Education, as I've experienced it, is casting artificial pearls before real swine.'

EIGHT

Industrial Relations

In July 1950 a questioner asked: 'In view of the constant labour unrest we are experiencing, is the working man fast becoming his own enemy?' It was Malcolm's first appearance on the programme and he replied very briefly.

In so far as the trade union movement is tending to allow itself to be used for political purposes, it is in fact proving to be the enemy of those in whose interest it's supposed to serve.

He was not much more voluble some five years later when discussing a strike at the Rolls-Royce factory in Scotland over the issue of an employee earning too much.

I think that one of the most dangerous elements in our present economic situation is the tendency of trade union power to be used to check work above the average. It is a terribly dangerous tendency and I think it is a tendency that one can observe in many unions and this particular dispute is a case of it. If you can arrive at the point in which the power of labour is so organised that the man who will work harder is penalised, then I think from the point of view of the general economy of the country you've arrived at a very dangerous situation.

During a shipyard strike in March 1957, much publicity was given to a statement by Ted Hill, General Secretary of the Boilermakers Union, that he was only concerned with his members and he put their interests before those of the country. The members of the team were asked to comment.

To tell you the truth, I rather liked Mr Hill's remark. I liked it because it was scrupulously honest and because he brushed aside a great deal of cant, which in this particular matter of wages I find wholly nauseating. Of course Mr Hill is concerned with the well-being of his trade union members – that's what he's paid to be. We don't expect stockbrokers not to invest in a very favourable share because it might be bad for the country; we assume that speculators in currency will sell sterling short if they think it's to their advantage, quite irrespective of the interests of the country. Even that very enlightened profession, doctors, are at the present moment agitating for more wages, and I don't suppose that as they lie awake in bed thinking about whether they're going to get it or not, the interests of the country loom very large.

The fact is that in an acquisitive society this is precisely what people do and I cannot for the life of me see how we can pick out Mr Hill for particular blame. This whole thing of wages has got buried in an awful morass of cant. I liked very much a joke drawing I saw once of the platform at the TUC and one of those trade union leaders with a very solid watch chain was standing up and he was saying, 'Hands up those in favour of higher wages.'

Malcolm also had some words of comfort for trade unionists when discussing, in October 1961, whether trade unions were being unreasonable in rejecting the Conservative Government's call for a pay pause in view of the economic situation.

The point is this: that if it were the case that dividends, that profits from industry, were going down, that would be another thing. But we all know that in point of fact they're tending to go up, and therefore it seems to me the height of humbug to say to people, 'You must not have higher wages because of an economic crisis, but at the same time of course it is in the national interest that industry should thrive.'

The fact is, you will never get any sense out of this wages business until you can control with utter rigidity and strength the rewards of industry of those who own it. If you could do that, then the argument about wages would apply, but as long as you don't, you're wasting your breath – on this programme or anywhere else – in saying to people, 'Now, we're in a tight hole, competition is very difficult, men must hold their wages down.' They'll never do it. And always, as long as you have a society which is based on the proposition that gain is the ultimate motive in human society, the man selling his labour will be as avid for gain as the man who is using his capital.

If you have a crisis like a war, then people will say, 'Well, in the national interest I'll do this and that.' But why do they do it? They do it because everybody is having to do the same thing. Now, if you go to the wage earner who is getting ten, fifteen, twenty pounds a week and you say to him, 'My dear friend, you're a patriot, we're all in this together, you mustn't have any more in order that we may thrive as a nation,' and you don't do it to the beneficiaries of industry – the management, the capitalist, the shareholder – this will be derisory.

I've had this argument in the only trade I know, which is printing, with men and they will say, 'Well, I'm not a great expert on balance sheets, but I did notice there was a very big profit in that enterprise. How can you have the face to say to me that I should moderate my demands if this is an enterprise which is bringing large profits to the people who own it?' This business of voluntary wage restriction will be cant and will never work unless and until you can rigorously and publicly and evidently control the profits that are derived from the work of those men in terms of dividends and managerial salaries and all the rest of it.

In June 1969, as on so many other occasions, there was a question about the current industrial unrest. 'What does it spring from?' a questioner asked.

There are different levels of unrest. The obvious one on the surface is simply that everybody wants higher wages. This is a very simple thing. If the BBC rang me up tomorrow and said, 'Next time you go on *Any Questions?* you'll be glad to hear that the fee's gone up by ten quid,' I should say, 'Oh, that's very nice.' Everybody's in that situation. Everybody wants higher wages and the only way they can get higher wages is by twisting the arm of the bosses, so they twist their arms and that's a strike.

Now, this is obviously not a very satisfactory arrangement, but then on the other hand, I think these are the surface things but underneath we are going through a phase of history of deep dissatisfaction with our way of life, precisely because we have largely lost sight of the only possible basis there can be for living – that is, that it is fulfilling some purpose greater than just living here and exercising our appetites and accumulating money or not accumulating it. That is, unfortunately, the attitude of people. Without being aware of it, they're in a mood to be troublesome and that's what it is.

How do you get that back? I don't know, except that people have to learn that that is so from bitter historical experience, and they will go through that bitter experience, probably quite soon.

After the Conservatives had won the general election of 1970, the Heath Government brought in the Industrial Relations Act and in June 1972 a questioner asked: 'Can it work?' Opposition to the Act had reached a climax in the case of the dockers who were sent to prison for defying the ruling of the Industrial Relations Court, only to be rescued by the Official Solicitor. The team also included Lord George-Brown.

The point is, if people realised it – which, of course, they don't – the whole system of law is in the process of breaking down because our society's breaking down. And therefore this particular law, which was duly passed by Parliament, has become completely farcical. A shop steward says, 'I'm not going to take any notice of this law,' and then another court says that in saying that, he hasn't put himself into contempt. Therefore one way and another I think it has become a total farce; but it's not alone in that. You'll find that more and more laws, as we go on, become both unobserved and farcical. That's how things break down.

GEORGE-BROWN: *I never thought bringing in the law was going to help, but somehow, somebody has got to bring back some order into our industrial situation – but the law won't do it.*

But, George, if the law can't do it, who is going to do it? Parliament obviously isn't, because Parliament's passed a Bill, and the Bill, by universal consent, has produced a farcical situation.

Lord George-Brown replied that it had to be a matter of persuasion and it was very tough.

Don't be fooled. This is not a matter of simply persuading people to be nice. There is here a defect in our society which Parliament has tried to correct and has failed. This is a very serious matter, and all the platitudes in the world in which you say, 'Of course, we are all going to be sensible and we want the right thing to happen,' won't get you by that difficulty. Today, in my opinion, is a very black day in our history. It's a day in which a law passed by Parliament and solemnly put on the Statute Book, was made totally farcical in the public eye. That is a more serious matter than people think.

A month later the Heath Government's difficulties with the unions were still a major talking point. A questioner asked: 'The present Government was elected with a clear mandate to bring the trade unions within the framework of the law. The unions are resisting this in every way they can. Is this behaviour compatible with a genuine belief in democracy?'

The answer to that must be 'No'. If Parliament passes an Act – whether it's a good Act or a bad Act is neither here nor there – and a section of society, whoever they may be, say, 'We are not going to take any notice of that Act, and we don't mind what you do to us, but we're still not going to take any notice of it,' – that is not compatible with genuine democracy as it has hitherto existed.

Now, the really serious aspect of this, which is seldom mentioned because it's a very awkward fact, is that the Government has not got the power, does not dispose of the power to cope with this anti-democratic action. In fact, they can't do anything about people who won't cooperate in working out this Act.

The truth is that, without our noticing it, we are moving into a condition of total lawlessness. This is a very serious matter. I'm not here saying that trade unions are wrong, or that the Act is good. But I am saying that, without noticing it, this is what is happening to us, and that, for instance, henceforth our newspapers will appear only by courtesy of certain trade unions participating. If at any minute they want to stop those papers, they can stop them, and the Government can do nothing about it. If it should so happen that any trade union wants to stop this radio programme – believe me, they could stop it and the Government could do nothing about it.

So we have reached a very serious crisis, a crisis in which our method of government does not work. I personally have been expecting this crisis for a long time, because I am firmly of the opinion that no society can run on a basis of competing greed. So my answer to this gentleman's question is, 'No, it is not compatible with genuine democracy, but I do not see what can be done about it in terms of governmental authority.'

A year later, in August 1973, a questioner drew attention to the vanishing work force. All forms of service were now depleted of staff. What could be done about it? Some of the team, which included Ted Willis, were in favour of higher wages, but Malcolm demurred.

It's easy to say 'Put up the wages' but surely the only result would be that the other wages would go up higher still. I mean, if you try to increase the gap between public assistance and earnings, then the pressures for raising public assistance will go up.

We have, in fact, for very honourable reasons, landed ourselves in an extraordinarily awkward situation and it would be quite dishonest of me to pretend that I see the answer. We are maintaining a sort of free enterprise economy but at the same time we have humanely removed all the arrangements which made that work, and therefore this process is likely to get more and more difficult.

I've been on many of these programmes over many years and always the same thing is said that has been said here – 'We must raise the wages.' Well, who doesn't want wages raised? This is an excellent thing and to a great extent it's happened, but at the same time it hasn't solved anything, and it won't solve anything until somehow or other you devise a way of living which is not based merely on trying to quite legitimately grab more and more. How you do that – of course, a doctrinaire socialist like old Ted would say you do it by having socialism, but he doesn't really believe that.

WILLIS: *How do you know?*

I'm quite sure that as the years go by, if *Any Questions?* continues – and we all hope it will continue for another twenty-five years – this question will from time to time be put and from time to time people will say, 'I think that the lower wages should be raised,' and we shall all applaud and we shall all feel what humane, good people we are, but we should have made no sort of contribution whatsoever to this particular problem.

In August 1975 when the programme was at Littlehampton in Sussex, a questioner asked what were the reasons for the apparent inability of the middle class in Great Britain to assert themselves, or to be seen to assert themselves. The team also included Lord Hailsham.

The reason that the middle class of this country don't assert themselves is because they have no power. The power in this country has been moved from them to – specifically – organised labour. And the middle classes cannot, through the ballot box or in any other way, assert themselves. They are in fact licked and they've got to accept it.

Lord Hailsham said he didn't feel licked at all; the middle class was going to win because each time a minority was attacked by the great Trade Union Congress or the Labour Party, they were going to stand together and they were going to beat them. This sentiment was greeted with rapturous applause by most of the audience.

I knew he'd get a colossal hand for that and it is utter rubbish. I'll tell you why, very briefly. Let him throw his mind back to when his government was in power and he was a member of it. A moment arose when there was a strike and the power stations were picketed by trade unionists. His party is predominantly a middle-class party, none the worse for that, but when it was in power and it was confronted by that situation, there was nothing it could do and it in effect capitulated. That is the proof, that's the answer to the question. If ever there was a time when, if they had any fight in them, they should have fought, that was it; and they capitulated, and they capitulated because they did not dispose of power sufficient to deal with the pickets by the power stations.

HAILSHAM: *Look what has happened since! The people will have more sense next time, they'll back us.*

Next time, next time – when are you going to get a next time?

They did, of course, get a next time and by September 1979, when a questioner asked: 'With growing storm clouds gathering, what advice would you give the Government to avoid further industrial conflict?' it was a Conservative government at the receiving end of the advice. The team also included John Junor, the Editor of the *Sunday Express*, and the Labour MP Eric Heffer.

I'm awfully sorry, but I don't know what the answer is to this question. To me, the situation is utterly and irretrievably hopeless. It's all very well to say, 'Let Leyland go bankrupt, let this go bankrupt, let that go bankrupt.' I quite see the point of that, but at the same time, of course, in fact it would destroy what's left of the economy of this country.

JUNOR: *Sorry, it wouldn't. Making Leyland bankrupt would not mean putting all the car workers out of jobs. It would mean that the viable sections of Leyland would continue.*

With all respect, John, I am very doubtful. I think if you left Leyland to sink or swim as best it could, there'd be awfully little of it left. It's possible that some of it could be salvaged, but the point is that first of all the Tory Government is not going to do that. You will find that the Tory Government will go on giving subsidies, because they too will not dare to risk large increases in unemployment brought about by the withdrawal of financial support, and they're probably wrong, but don't imagine that what you say is going to come to pass, because it won't.

Our economy is in an absolutely appalling doom. The various circumstances that have led to that, we might have differences of opinion about. I mean, dear Eric says, 'We'll sit down at a table and work out a reasonable settlement with the trade union leaders.' Dear God, how many hours and hours and hours have been spent sitting at tables with those same men. We have reached, in the economic life of the society we belong to, a sort of impasse in which each side offers this: Eric says, 'Sit down and talk to these trade union leaders.' John says, 'Let the ones that are going bust go bust. Let's get rid of the people who don't want to work, etc.' None of this is in any way practical. People have sat down and talked with trade unions and, you're quite right, they will have to go on talking to the trade union leaders, but they won't get anywhere. We've reached a point where there is not an answer. If you make a law to deal with it, the law will not be observed.

NINE

Party Politics

In March 1952 a questioner asked: 'In view of the virtual extinction of the Parliamentary Liberal Party, does the team agree that the small number of Liberal MPs in the present House of Commons would serve a better purpose if they amalgamated with either the Conservative or the Labour Party?'

I find it a very difficult question to answer, partly because when a political party is becoming extinct, does it really matter what it does? I mean, if we consider the voting of the Liberal Party during the last decade, we shall find that it has been on almost every occasion, until very recently, divided in two and that as such it has completely cancelled itself out.

Now presumably if it divided and joined the two great parties it would join them in approximately equal numbers and we should be just where we were. So that as Liberalism has become a sort of – not exactly a joke, but it has been something we have all got used to, I cannot see really why it should not go on, playing this curious role of dividing itself on every occasion equally between the two parties.

In October 1954 the team was asked: 'If Keir Hardie were alive today would he be a supporter of Attlee or Bevan?' It was Labour Party Conference time, during a period when Aneurin Bevan was a rebel against the official Opposition policy under the leadership of Clement Attlee.

I have attended a great many Labour Party Conferences sitting in the reporters' gallery, and we always used to exchange a look up there when anybody got up and said, 'If Keir Hardie were alive today...' because we always knew we were going to hear some even greater baloney than the normal speech.

My own opinion is that if Keir Hardie were alive today, he would be an eager and active member of the Right Wing of the Conservative Party.

In April 1955 a questioner asked whether those who didn't vote should lose the right to vote.

I'm absolutely sure they shouldn't be disenfranchised. What is more, I think that the people who don't vote are the absolute flower of our community. They are the élite, they are the people who have realised the only fundamental truth, which is that though these politicians in their personal capacity are nearly always the most enchanting people, in their public capacity they're a lot of rogues, and equally rogues, and the realisation of that point naturally induces one not to vote for either of them.

In December 1957 a questioner asked: 'Earl Ferrers is reported to have said that he finds women in politics highly distasteful. Does the team agree?' The team included the Labour MP Barbara Castle.

It's a little delicate to discuss this question in the presence of so charming a person as Mrs Castle. I would duck the issue slightly by pointing out that the best governed and probably the most prosperous country in the world today is Switzerland, where woman have not yet been given the vote. That, I think, is a highly significant fact. Nor would I think that on the whole women in politics have been notably successful. When you think that the majority of the British electorate is female, it's astonishing that so few women have been, in fact, elected.

Perhaps Earl Ferrers put it a little strongly, but I think he's got an idea there.

In 1959 the Conservatives won the general election with a thumping majority, and in May of the following year a questioner asked: 'The nation has shown considerable confidence in the policy of the Conservative Party both at the general election and more recently in the municipal elections; in view of this, what suggestions would the team make to the leaders of the other parties?'

It seems to me that the situation is really extraordinary because you have, in effect, a Conservative Party without a policy and a policy without a Labour Party. And when one thinks of the leader of the Labour Party, Mr Gaitskell, and what he's going to do, one realises that these must be very anxious moments for him, because if he borrows what he supposes to be the policy which would enable him to win a general election, then a lot of his own party are against him. If, on the other hand, he falls in with their wishes, he is more or less certain that he can't win an election. So this poor Mr Gaitskell is in a very unhappy situation. And I would think, as we were asked to give advice, that really the best thing he could do would be to keep quite quiet for a bit and see what happens.

Malcolm's advice was clearly sound, because Labour won the next election, and as Hugh Gaitskell had since died, Harold Wilson became Prime Minister. He had a second general election victory in 1966 but was not without his critics in the Labour Party. After the Party Conference in October 1968, a questioner asked if the team thought Wilson had regained the party's confidence.

Every single figure in our time simply gets into power and does the exact opposite of what he said he was going to do and receives this fantastic applause. The most extraordinary example, of course, is de Gaulle, but Wilson is running him up.

There was a general election on 28 February 1974 and the result was a real cliff-hanger — so much so, that it was several days before Harold Wilson was firmly back in Downing Street, ousting Edward Heath. With a tiny majority, the new Prime Minister had many problems in governing the country

and by August a questioner was asking the team: 'Has the country become ungovernable, other than by a military or left-wing dictatorship?'

I certainly think it's very far along the path of being ungovernable. The whole economic and political system is breaking down. Whether you could imagine in this country a left-wing or right-wing ideological dictatorship or a military dictatorship I'm extremely doubtful and I think it's much more likely that what lies before us in the immediate future is what's happening in Italy, which is just a slow, and then a little faster, total breakdown.

I was very interested to see that there they don't only not deliver the mail – everybody's got used to that – but they actually sell it off for pulp when it accumulates beyond a certain point. So you might be going along and suddenly see your letter to Auntie Mabel being pulped.

I think that's what lies ahead of us because never, observing public affairs, not even in 1940 when things looked very bleak, have I had such a sense of our country being literally on the edge of an abyss.

I think it's important to notice, if you look over the world, how very small is the part of the world left where even an effort is being made to govern in this way. Every single one, for instance, of the new regimes in Africa, every single one is a dictatorial regime in which the party in power puts the opposition in prison or otherwise disposes of them, having got their independence on the slogans 'Majority rule' and 'One man, one vote'. Apart from Western Europe, really all the rest of it is dictatorially governed. Asia – you have a very groggy sort of democracy in India, otherwise a dictatorial regime. And I think there's some significance in that even the effort is only being made in a tiny little corner of the world, and it's getting increasingly difficult even to pretend that it's working in that part.

A few weeks later Harold Wilson went to the country and got the increased majority he needed. Having lost two general elections in one year, Edward Heath was in due course replaced as Leader of the Conservative Party by Margaret Thatcher. In January 1976 the team was asked what Mrs Thatcher must do as leader to revitalise the Opposition.

My true opinion is that the Conservative Party no longer wants power, and they no longer want power because they haven't the faintest idea what to do about the only really important issue that arises – that is to say, how to deal with the trade unions.

I would say myself, imagining as I sometimes do that I might be a historian years hence writing about this last harlequinade of our Western civilisation, that the choice of Mrs Thatcher and of the people round her will be seen historically as representing a desire not to have power and I sympathise with them because, as Mr Heath showed when he had a majority, he was totally unable to deal with militant trade unions and I'm absolutely sure Mrs Thatcher certainly has given no conceivable notion of how she would set about it, beyond producing a certain number of rather tiresome platitudes.

Therefore I think Mr Wilson's government is perfectly safe unless they come to grief within themselves or by finally alienating the Scottish Nationalists, who may well, before very long, hold the balance of power.

In the spring of 1977 there was a by-election in the Stetchford division of Birmingham and the vote for the National Front candidate showed an increase. A questioner in

April asked if this increased vote was an indication of a revival of Fascism in this country. The team included Freddie Laker.

If it's Fascism, it's quite a definite and explicit thing; we know exactly what it is. It's commending a certain type of authoritarian government and a certain manner of conducting our affairs. I would have doubted whether these four thousand votes in Birmingham were entirely due to very strong feelings about racialism there which are in a certain degree perfectly understandable. And if that finds this very ugly expression – well, you find of course exactly the same sort of thing among university students who are supported by the State and who refuse to allow someone like Keith Joseph to come and speak to them, yell and shout and howl, exactly the same thing, and actually get away with it which is rather disconcerting.

There are various things that are going on which are highly repellent to large numbers of people, but it's no good just fastening on the National Front and saying, 'There's Hitlerism rising up again.' It's something that's happening, and it's happening in quarters like universities where it's least justifiable because if you pay a lot of money for higher education it should at least produce people who are reasonable, who want to understand things. They are to me far more reprehensible than what is going on in this former constituency of Roy Jenkins. I think you've got to face the fact, and it's a disagreeable fact, that in the present circumstances this is cropping up in many quarters and that it is not Fascism, it is simply hooliganism.

LAKER: *I'm totally opposed to any form of extremism, whether it be Left or Right. I don't believe that there's a revival of Fascism in this country any more than I think that Communism is going to go a long way. On the other hand, I feel that the whole nation, and it certainly includes me, is in rebellion. We have nowhere to go, we have no leadership, and some people on the fringe will be attracted by all sorts of funny parties like the National Front. We're always going to get some extreme right wingers, like left wingers, but this is all bred out of the natural rebellion that we have throughout the country today.*

There are so many politicians, there are 635 of the blighters, all earning too much money for what they do. If I had my way, I'd reduce the number by at least seventy-five per cent, I'd pay them £30,000 a year and non-attendance money.

You talk about natural rebellion, Freddie. The proper response that you ought to make, and the people ought to make, to that feeling is to get yourself elected to Parliament, to take part in the political business. It's no good just saying, 'We're all being misled, we're all in a terrible mess, we're all angry.' If we are to enjoy having a democratic system of government, then there are an infinite number of means whereby people who feel as you do can express that other than by merely shouting, and shouting other people down.

You see, it's no good just saying here, 'Yes, this is going on and it's a shocking thing and if only we could stop Members of Parliament going to Parliament everything would be better.' It wouldn't. It would be worse.

TEN

Overseas Affairs

In March 1957 a questioner asked: 'Does the team consider that Archbishop Makarios's return to Cyprus might now be a bridge towards better relations or a time bomb which might cause an even more dangerous explosion later on?' The others discussing the Archbishop's return from exile included Jack Longland.

One thing I'm quite sure of is that Archbishop Makarios will return to Cyprus and we shall negotiate with him because every time, ever since Ireland became independent Eire, every time that we've said that we will never negotiate with that man, we always have and he nearly always finishes up by being prime minister. So that if I were an ambitious Cypriot or Mauritian, or from one of these territories that still have not yet been given what's laughingly called their independence, I would immediately get myself exiled, knowing that by doing that it was absolutely certain that in a relatively short time I'd become head of the whole show.

Also, I would like to remind you that there is another factor in this island of Cyprus and that is the Turkish population there, which consists, I believe, of about one-fifth of it; and these people, far from being delighted by the return of Archbishop Makarios, are going to be extremely annoyed.

The point is that we've landed ourselves in a very, very awkward position. I quite agree with what Longland said about the complete futility of regarding Cyprus as a base – it never could have been a base and it's proved that it can't be a base – but unfortunately we've landed ourselves in a political mess there to which there is no cut and dried solution. Merely bringing back this Archbishop is not in itself going to solve the thing.

Four years later, there were demonstrations in London over the death in prison of Patrice Lumumba, first Prime Minister of the independent Congo, and the members of the team were asked for their reactions.

I wasn't a friend of Lumumba's but I regret the old boy's passing. It seems to me a sad thing that he should have been bumped off, but in view of the enormous number of people in our time who have been bumped off in various countries, I find this a little difficult to feel particular indignation about. Furthermore, I am temperamentally opposed to demonstrations. There have been demonstrations during my lifetime about all sorts of things and all sorts of people. It seems to me that in this question of Africa, you have these countries emerging, as after the Middle Ages countries emerged in Europe, and there is bound to be a great deal of struggle and conflict and fighting and murder.

Now, Lumumba invited the United Nations to come in; but he also asked them to go out. He was a rather whimsical character and if I'd still been editor of *Punch* I should even more regret his passing than I do now, but I can't feel that going through the streets of London and saying 'What a wicked thing to kill Lumumba' really achieved anything, because the murder of Lumumba is a factor of this appalling, complicated situation that has arisen in the Congo. His men killed a lot of people and the others killed a lot of his people, and ultimately they killed him.

I would like to live in a world in which people weren't killed, but by an ill chance I happen to have lived in one in which some millions of people have been killed by all sorts of governments, and I find it difficult to concentrate particular moral indignation on this particular incident. Of course, it's quite obvious that Lumumba will be built up into a sort of Gladstone of the Congo. But it won't be true and, as such, I find the whole thing rather unreal.

In June 1969 a questioner asked: 'Should Gibraltar be given back to Spain?' Malcolm, once again, was the last member of the team to contribute.

There are three points that I'd add. The first is that we grabbed the Rock of Gibraltar for strategic reasons. Presumably it has no strategic reasons any more, so that can be ruled out.

Secondly, what nobody mentions is that the United Nations has in fact decreed that it must be handed back to Spain. Now, I've noticed a curious thing – that the people who are very keen on intervening in Rhodesia always plead the United Nations; they say, '*They* say we must do it, so we must do it.' But those same people keep singularly silent about the fact that the United Nations, with the approval of the Communist countries – who don't in the least mind the Rock apparently going back to a sort of Fascist regime – have in fact told us to do it, so that is left out of account.

Thirdly, I would say that it's perfectly obvious that the British people don't give twopence either way. If they did, it is inconceivable that they would all go and replenish the

Spanish economy by taking their holidays along the Costa Brava. The last time this thing cropped up, a pathetic appeal was made by the Foreign Secretary that patriotic Britons should not go to Spain for a holiday. There was absolutely no response whatever. So I assume from that – and probably rightly – that the English are utterly indifferent what happens to this rock, but of course they may very well be concerned about the twenty-five thousand people who live there and I have very little doubt they will be installed in this country before very long.

In September 1971 a questioner asked: 'Do events in Ireland and elsewhere suggest that partition is a device by which one generation transfers its intractable problems to the next?' Another member of the team, Douglas Hurd, a future Foreign Office Minister in Mrs Thatcher's government, said it was a device by which one generation stops its members from slaughtering each other and he cited Ireland, Palestine, India and Pakistan.

Young Hurd, you've been indoctrinated by the current myth. To say that India and Pakistan were divided to stop slaughter – do you know how many people were slaughtered through the partition? Three million. The point is that these partitions are done because politicians can't think of a proper answer, and each of them leaves behind a hideous legacy to which in fact there is no answer. In the case of India and Pakistan, in order to get out quickly we allowed this ridiculous partition to take place, which never had the remotest chance of working. In the Middle East, in order to get out of a mandate that we could no longer execute, we left a situation there to which there is no solution, and similarly in

Ireland. And what in fact these dreadful situations are, are the harvest of devices adopted by the politicians of the time to evade solving a problem that confronts them.

These trouble-spots were created by those in authority, namely politicians, not working out a proper solution. If you take the case of India and Pakistan, the division of that country, of India, which took place and that frontier that was drawn, anybody who knew anything about it knew that this was an absolutely intolerable arrangement and we should not have withdrawn from India to leave such a miserable state of affairs behind. That's the real truth of it.

In November 1974 the team was asked whether there should be a United Nations peace-keeping force in Northern Ireland.

I think that a United Nations peace-keeping force would have to be so huge to maintain order there that the United Nations would be quite unable to provide it. That's point number one. I don't think it is a practical suggestion for a United Nations force to undertake the very disagreeable duty that is now being done by British forces. And frankly, I see no end to this tragic situation. I was there the other day and I came away with a very depressing feeling.

Finally, I would like to make the point that everybody says this is a row between Irish Catholics and Irish Protestants. My experience of it, such as it is through one or two television interviews and things like that, is that Protestantism and Catholicism as such are an extraordinarily small part. Once I had to interview Cardinal Conway and the Anglican Archbishop and the Moderator there, and we didn't make much progress until I said to them, 'Now, supposing you went out tonight to the barricades and told your people to go home, to leave the barricades, would they go?' and with one accord they said, 'Of course they wouldn't.'

So, you see, there is really something rather mystical about this talking of Protestants and Catholics. It's much more a question, on the surface, of Irish nationalism in the South and British nationalism in the North and underneath that, in my opinion, as will be seen, is much more a revolutionary movement which will probably, if and when the troops are withdrawn, engulf the whole country.

The problem of Ireland came up again in September 1979, this time on a different basis. The question was: 'In view of the Republic of Ireland's attitude to security problems, are we still justified in allowing its citizens unrestricted entry to this country, and voting rights and other benefits when they're here?' The team also included John Junor.

This business in Northern Ireland is another thing that I have to say in all honesty I haven't got any ready answer to at all. I should think that controlling the Irish people coming here would be an enormously difficult business, because the passage of people, the number of people working here and settled here, many of whom couldn't easily be dispensed with, would present appalling difficulties. I question very much whether it would be possible to put a security control on traffic between the Republic of Ireland and here.

There are two things that could be done about the situation in Northern Ireland. One would be to say, 'This country is part of England and we will therefore fortify the frontier – protect it as we would British territory,' and on that basis it could be done, but we haven't got the resources to do that. We haven't got the men to do it and we haven't got the will to do it.

Alternatively, we could say to the people in Northern Ireland, 'We can't do that – we can't, in fact, defend you. We can't incorporate you into Britain; we can't protect you from this' – which we can't – 'and therefore we're sending down somebody to see what terms he can make with the Government in Dublin.'

Those are the only two courses that are open to us. Neither of them will be done. And so we shall flounder on from year to year to year, having these miserable episodes like the murder of Mountbatten, and considering possibilities of doing this and doing that, hearing Mrs Thatcher, or some successor of hers, say on the air, 'We really must make security better.' Well, what's the good of saying that?

John Junor said that the Republic of Ireland was a foreign country; there should be a border and the border probably ought to be mined.

Do you believe it's practical politics to fortify that long land frontier in such a way that it wouldn't be possible for people to do what they did when those seventeen soldiers were killed? To set off an explosion from the Republic territory?

JUNOR: *From the other side of the border...*

So that they don't even have to hide. They can just do it. Do you imagine that that is a situation to which there's any end?

In December 1977, nearly four years before his assassination, President Sadat of Egypt made his momentous journey to Jerusalem in an attempt to ease the tension between Israel and the Arab States. A questioner asked whether his journey had paved the way to peace or increased the danger of war.

I hate to be a damper but I don't think it's had any effect whatsoever. In the last fifty years, working as a journalist, I've been watching these gestures being made, like when Chamberlain went to see Hitler and came back and waved his piece of paper and said that we'd agreed never to fight, that Britain and Germany were not going to fight. Everybody went mad with excitement, as they did about Sadat, and said 'How wonderful!' The thing is, these general declarations don't get us anywhere. Politics are about power and they have to be settled in terms of power.

Now, neither Sadat nor the Premier of Israel has made any sort of suggestion which could possibly lead to a solution to the present difficulties in the Middle East, which are simply that the Arabs demand back their territory. If they're given their territory, Israel ceases to exist; therefore Israel is not prepared to cede this territory. Nothing has happened in all this dementia which alters that in any way.

I have learned through journalism, through watching these things going on. All the countries that were attacked by the Soviet Union after the war, during the war, were countries which had a non-aggression pact. I remember the Kellogg Pact, when every nation in the world went for it and signed a peace treaty saying, 'We will never go to war.' Well, these things are totally meaningless. Politics, diplomacy, are about power. When Sadat makes some concrete proposal about recognising Israel, when Israel makes some concrete response to that, then I shall become interested.

ELEVEN

The Family and the Law

In May 1965 a questioner asked the team to discuss a proposal by the judge Sir Jocelyn Symonds that there should be no divorce between couples with children under seventeen and that childless couples should receive divorce by consent. Ralph Wightman, an agricultural journalist who was a regular member of the team for many years, commented that things would be made worse for the children if parents who hated each other were forced to remain together.

I think that Sir Jocelyn Symonds is one of the very few men who sit on a judge's bench who's really said something sensible. This is most unusual, because most judges talk drivel the whole time.

I think it's a most excellent idea because after all, in the first place, children need two parents. Now, Ralph says 'parents who hate each other'. This is a relative term. All married couples have their ups and downs and if they knew that, having brought children into the world, they were duty bound to look after them until they were old enough to go out into the world, this in my opinion would be an excellent thing.

In point of fact, I don't think there's any point in having divorces at all for two reasons: one is, in my experience, people who divorce one wife or husband always immediately afterwards marry the identical person – they choose a husband or wife exactly the same, and they're exactly where they were, except that a lot of trouble and expense has been gone to. Then, of course, adultery is always available if people don't want to be faithful – as we know, there are quite a lot of people who do that.

Finally, in the case of childless marriages, what does it matter to us or to society whether they stay together or whether they don't? The point of marriage is to bring children into the world; the responsibility of people who marry is to bring those children up and that, from society's point of view, is the beginning and end of the whole set-up.

In May 1967 a questioner asked: 'One child in six doesn't have enough to eat and lives in extreme poverty; with the present level of allowances, is some of the alleged poverty due to parents having their priorities wrong, especially in relation to family limitation?'

This business of poverty and malnutrition is one that I hesitate to speak dogmatically about because the whole thing is relative. I mean, the poorest person in this country is a sort of millionaire compared with the majority of people in countries like India.

We all know there are people who don't have enough material things, but the precise level of material things that (a) are required to sustain life, and (b) are due to people, is extremely difficult to fix, and I think there's a lot of ill-judged talk about it, based on the fallacious assumption that it's possible to set out statistically exactly what people ought to have or what they haven't got.

With regard to the question of limitation of families, the implication of the questioner is that people have too many children. I find this a most offensive suggestion. Driving my car here today, I heard some ghastly little BBC interviewer saying to a lady who had nine children, 'Now do you think you ought to have had all these children?' I was waiting for the lady to hoof her out of the room but unfortunately she didn't. But the point is that this idea that when people are poor it's because they've had too many children is one that when I was young was one of the means whereby the rich salved their consciences about people like Irish peasants and so on. I think it's a sheer impertinence to suggest that people should be forced to have fewer children than they want to have.

This notion of a population explosion is one of those mumbo-jumbo phrases of our time which is based on absolutely no scientific reality whatever. It's a pure piece of humbug. If we were to use the resources that are now available to produce food and to make the unproductive parts of the world productive, there would be no occasion to say that there were too many people. There are not too many people. There is too much selfish use of what we have.

Now, we spend on producing weapons of destruction a vast sum of money. America and Russia spend even more. Supposing just for one moment that a mood of sanity could afflict the strange race that we all belong to, supposing that we were able tomorrow to turn over to productive purposes the skills and the wealth and the technological knowledge which goes into making these weapons of destruction, to making the earth fruitful, then talking about a population explosion would be completely nonsensical. We talk about a population explosion because we have neither the moral courage nor the physical courage to use the resources that exist to hand in the world to feed the people who need to be fed.

History books will judge us, our generation, who sit whimpering about a population explosion when we have these fantastic means of production which we don't use, and are even able to explore the universe itself through our technological knowledge. We sit snivelling in our places and say there are too many people – history books would judge us very savagely.

In February 1977 the members of the team were asked whether they agreed with a judge's lenient attitude towards youths charged with having illegal sexual relationships with under-aged girls, particularly the view expressed that immorality should be no concern of the Courts.

I'll tell you what strikes me about this thing. What is the law? I am not interested in what this judge thinks about how young people should behave or what is right. Frankly, it doesn't interest me. I don't think very much of judges and I wouldn't attach great importance to anything they said. He is employed and paid a large salary to administer the law.

Now, if he says, 'These two people have broken the law but I, a judge, decide that it doesn't matter' – which is in fact what he said, and 'Don't imagine that because you have come to the Old Bailey you have broken a law, you didn't do any such thing; you simply obeyed a very reasonable appetite,' then I think he ought to be turned off the bench, that's my view.

I think – I am quite serious about this – I think it has gone much too far, with judges talking about the law and saying, 'You haven't really ...'; and this applies particularly to something – a phrase that turns my blood cold – which is called 'mercy killing'. When judges say, 'Yes, you murdered that person, but in my opinion that was an act of great charity and I don't think anything should happen to you.'

This man – what he said was, 'Don't imagine because you have been brought here to the Old Bailey on this charge that there is anything wrong, anything for you to be ashamed of' – that is what he said, that's what I object to. I don't care if he punishes them or not, that's a separate issue. But he takes it upon himself to say, 'The law says so-and-so, you have broken the law, but of course that's all right, don't worry about that.' I think this is very dangerous.

In September 1979 a questioner asked whether in view of recent discussions about lowering the age of consent, the team considered children under the age of sixteen would be able to cope with such a liberated situation.

This is a very wicked and undesirable proposition and, while it is extremely unlikely to come to pass, there's something in it for my money which is even more sinister than that. That is the assumption on which it's based. The assumption is that since children unfortunately are behaving promiscuously at an earlier age than the age of consent, therefore the age of consent should be adjusted to fall in with their practice. In other words, there is no morality, there is no good and evil, there is merely what is at a given moment acceptable to the majority of people. And I think this is a formula for complete moral disintegration of a society.

The same argument, you see, is applied to marijuana, to the legalisation of marijuana. People are smoking marijuana, *ergo* marijuana must be legalised. Now, anyone who's lived and taught in the Middle East, as I have, knows what hashish does to a population. I assure you, when I was teaching at Cairo University forty years ago, you wouldn't have found one single person, Egyptian, European or anybody else, who would for a second have thought that hashish was other than an appalling, disastrous addiction. Now you have to listen to all sorts of life peeresses and drivelling people of that kind saying that marijuana is harmless and this diabolical argument again coming up that because it is a fact that large numbers of children are smoking marijuana, therefore we must legalise it. You go on applying that, and you destroy completely the basis of all morality.

When Solzhenitsyn arrived in the West and he said that what is wrong with the West is that they've forgotten about good and evil, what an extraordinarily perceptive remark that was, because it's absolutely true.

TWELVE

Humour

Malcolm was editor of *Punch* from 1953 to 1957 and during this period he must have steeled himself to encounter questions like the one in March 1957: 'Are the jokes in *Punch* as funny as they used to be?'

This is an extremely painful question, as you no doubt will understand, because I am inclined to agree with the questioner that the jokes are not as funny as they used to be. But the only thing that comforts me is that I look at old volumes of *Punch* and I find they never used to be, either. So the situation really is very much as it was.

The truth is, however, that it is becoming increasingly difficult to be funny about the world we live in because the world itself is getting so much funnier than anything you could possibly think of. Now, may I suggest to you, how is it possible to be funny about Mr John Foster Dulles?* He's uproariously funny himself. How is it possible, for that matter, to be funny about the British Broadcasting Corporation, which is an institution so full of humour that every time you try and make a joke about it, you find the Corporation itself has beaten you to it.

Now, I'll tell you one tiny incident that illustrates what I mean. We thought once that it would be a good idea to do a parody of the *Radio Times* – take a page and make a parody

*US Secretary of State

of it, and we went to it with a will and we thought we'd worked out one or two quite funny things. But the member of my staff who was mainly responsible for doing it came to me in a state of great agitation just before this parody was going to appear, with a copy of the *Radio Times*, pointing out to me that they'd beaten us because do you know what there was? There was a talk in the Third Programme on 'The place of the potato in British folklore'.

If anybody here can succeed in being funnier than that, I offer a job on *Punch* at a very munificent salary immediately.

In October 1961 the team was asked: 'The Northerners are usually regarded with some contempt by the Southerners; how do you account for the great success of many Northern comedians?' This question immediately followed one about public schools.

Over the question of Northern people being despised, this goes back to the previous question. People look down on them because they don't speak in this particular sort of bastard English which has been produced by the public schools and the BBC – that's the origin of them being despised.

Over them being comedians – I speak of this with some feeling, as a man who was for five sombre years editor of what purported to be a humorous paper – you find that in many ways the North-countryman and the person from the Dominions are better as humorists because humour, like all good things, depends entirely on truth. Good jokes are true. Bad jokes are false. And there is a certain predisposition on the part of North-country people, with whom I'd associate Canadians, Australians, people like that, to be rather more truthful and therefore they're funnier, they're not trying to evade things. Bad humour is an evasion of reality. Good humour is an acceptance of it.

In May 1967 the team was asked to what extent the great English eccentrics had been engendered by the eccentricity of the English climate. As was pointed out later by another member of the team, Malcolm failed to answer the question, but spoke engagingly on the subject of English eccentrics and again harked back to his grisly experience as editor of *Punch*.

In the days when I was editor of this magazine, peers and clergymen were our absolute standby. In those days, every time I read that there was a threat of closing the House of Lords, or every time I read that the number of ordinands in the Church of England was falling, my heart used to sink because I thought, 'If they fall below a certain point, and if they shut down the House of Lords, we might as well pack up.'

Now, why should these two classes of people, peers and clergymen, provide this reservoir of eccentricity? I suggest there's a very simple explanation. It is because neither of them have anything to do. So that I would attribute English eccentricity, in so far as it exists, entirely to the fact that we have nurtured to our bosom these two categories of relatively educated individuals and then given them nothing whatever to do, and in this way we have ensured a ready supply of eccentricity.

Now the question is this: is this supply going to keep up? Because I notice certain alarming things. In the first place, in the House of Lords they're beginning to suggest they should do things, and that, of course, is very, very frightening because we shall lose our eccentricity if that happens. As for the clergy, apart from the fact that their numbers are dwindling, there's also a certain tendency among them to take their religion seriously. Now, this could cut the ground from under both a great category of humour and also a great reservoir of eccentricity and I hope it won't go any further than it has.

In June 1969 the members of the team were asked if they considered that humour must always contain some slight tinge of malice.

The truth is that this quest for good-natured, jolly humour is a vain pursuit. Humour is really like a sort of mysticism, it's the opposite face of mysticism and it expresses the sense of imperfection that we have as human beings, and therefore in that sense it's bound to be critical. Humour is an expression, in terms of the grotesque, of the inconceivable disparity between human aspiration and human performance. Now, that definition is particularly good because it explains to us why sex is so funny. Sex is enormously funny, and I tell you something – as you get older it gets funnier and funnier. That's something to send you home happy, and the point is that of all conceivable human activities, that is the one which most demonstrates this disparity between human aspiration and human performance. That's why it's so funny.

THIRTEEN

The Common Market

Visiting the carpet factory at Axminster in December 1957, the team was asked why the carpet trade should be exposed to competition while farmers were protected.

I've read various things about this European Free Trade scheme without being able to get any clear idea of what is proposed, and I don't think anybody knows because the thing is still in a state of considerable confusion. But it seems to me that in principle it's a good idea, because I question very much whether a whole series of little sovereign states in Western Europe, each pursuing its own narrow economic interests, will be able to survive in the world as we know it today. In other words, there might have to be sacrifices, certain industries might suffer, but in general I'm absolutely confident that Western Europe will only go on existing as a viable economic proposition to the extent that it becomes more or less a common economic area.

Uncertainty over the details of the Common Market still persisted in Malcolm's mind ten years later. In May 1967 he faced the question: 'If we pay to enter and pay more for food, what advantages do we get from the Common Market?'

As a hater of mass communication media, it interests me to notice that over the last – it seems to me – hundred years, but it can't be more than three or four, all the mass communication media have been going hard out to tell me what the Common Market's about, but I'm totally unable to understand anything about it; and I find to my great pleasure in talking to my countrymen that most of them are in precisely the same situation. In other words, this vast outpouring of words has simply not taken in any way, and I was reinforced in this opinion because a couple of years ago CBC Television asked me to go and stand on the frontier between Belgium and Holland with a microphone in my hand and ask people passing through the frontier what they thought about the Common Market.

Well, I stood there – it was rather a rainy day, a rather cold day, and there I was standing microphone in hand, and believe me or not, I couldn't find a living soul who'd ever heard of it. Nor was there the slightest difference that I could detect in the degree of customs examination, passport examination, in fact the whole thing may very well be one of those strange fantasies.

I am inclined to think that this must be so, because in announcing that we were going to try and get in again, the Prime Minister said – in that portentious way that all politicians cultivate on such occasions – he said that the decisions that we are taking may well shape our national life and the life of Europe for centuries to come. Now, whenever a politician says that, you can be absolutely certain – and I speak as a journalist of forty years' standing – you can be absolutely certain that nothing whatever will happen.

Another seven years elapsed and Malcolm's early faith in the idea of a European Common Market seemed to have been

lost. In May 1974 the members of the team were asked what they thought about the prospects for the development of unity within the Common Market, in view of the departure of the West German Chancellor Willy Brandt, the election of a new President in France, and Mr Callaghan's proposed renegotiation of the terms of Britain's entry into the EEC.

I'm afraid I never had the slightest belief or hope in the possibility of any form of unity within the Common Market, nor did I ever believe that it was a serious project, and I think that events have proved that this is so. The reason is that it attempted to achieve unity through relating self-interest of the component countries to one another. Unity is never achieved in this way. Unity is only achieved through having a common faith and a common purpose. And I think that the thing was from the beginning what the late lamented Mussolini used to call 'a big lemonade' and is likely to remain so until it finally sinks into oblivion, rather like the Holy Roman Empire.

I think that cultivated prime ministers talking in a nice way in English, recognising differences – this is not unity, this is not what 'united' meant. Men unite over their beliefs and nothing but beliefs, and there's no belief in this. It's purely a matter of a certain type of economic organisation that will neither bring us the unity nor strength, however rich, however successful it might be. In fact, it has been a total flop.

Three years later, in July 1977, the members of the team were asked for their opinion of the Common Market with relation to food prices on the one hand and our farming community on the other, and Malcolm was no more enthusiastic.

Personally, I have no belief in the Market at all. It sounds rather ridiculous really, but to me it's a kind of fantasy thing. I don't think it has any reality and indeed many of the things that have been set up in the twentieth century – SEATO, CENTO, NATO, UNESCO, all these different things – seem to me to be fantasies.

When I was a child we lived near a pub and one of the things I used to watch was when the pub was turning out at ten o'clock, and it would very often happen that ten or a dozen people would emerge from the pub in a state of different degrees of inebriation, and they would hold on to each other in order to prevent falling over. Now, that's how I see the Common Market, and I noticed that three new drinkers, namely Portugal, Spain and Greece, are going to join that swaying group of people holding desperately on to each other in order not to fall flat on their faces.

FOURTEEN

Animals

In the autumn of 1956 there were some people in Great Britain who appeared to be less concerned over the Russian invasion of Hungary than they were over the Russian use of dogs in experiment in space travel. Malcolm, then Editor of *Punch*, made it clear that he did not share this view when he discussed the matter in December.

I have professionally to try and sometimes think of jokes and there are always things happening in the world which deeply humiliate me because they're so much funnier than anything you can think of; and I must say that in view of what's been going on in this unhappy world of ours of recent decades and in recent years and, alas, in recent weeks in places like Hungary, the idea that estimable people should get extremely agitated and indignant about the use of dogs in a rocket struck me as ineffably and ironically funny.

There is one trifling incident that's connected with this that's imperishably planted in my mind. At the time of one of the atomic tests in the United States – I was a correspondent in Washington – they took a lot of animals down there and these animals came back, the ship came back, and we were invited on board the ship to go and see them. They were living in great luxury and ease; one couldn't help feeling a tiny bit envious of them. But there was one that took my fancy very much – it was labelled as a neurotic goat. And they investigated the reaction of this neurotic goat to an atomic explosion and the conclusion that was reached was that the goat was neither more nor less neurotic as a result of the explosion.

Nine years later, in May 1965, Malcolm took a more serious view of animal welfare. The question concerned animals who were specially bred for scientific purposes but this in no way discouraged him from talking about factory farming.

This attitude that we are developing to animals is growing very dangerous, because ultimately what it expresses is a lack of respect for life. And the one thing you must do with life is respect it. Now, if you take animals and do this factory system with them – all right, you make all these arguments and you say that this is a more economical way of producing food and therefore we must do it. But some time someone is going to say, 'That's a more economical way of bringing up men; let's do the same thing to them,' and the logic would in fact be unanswerable. And I myself, though I know nothing about it technically, feel an instinctive loathing of this idea that animals must be treated with complete contempt in order that they may serve men, and I think you'll find it'll have terrible consequences.

Malcolm had another opportunity of talking about intensive farming methods in June 1969, when a questioner

asked what should be done about them. The team also
included the actor Brian Rix.

What should be done? Well, I think the first thing is –
which I have in fact done myself – one shouldn't eat meat.
Because if you don't eat meat then you at least detach yourself
from something which is peculiarly abhorrent. Now, why is it
abhorrent? Brian makes the point that after all if you have
animals in the fields they aren't there for so very long and
they're killed. I think there's an enormous difference between
animals in fields and animals in factory farms, and the basic
difference lies in this: the one thing you have to do with
human life, or you perish, is to respect it. You must respect
every aspect of it. Even the contours of the hills you must
respect. Everything.

Now, to take an animal and, in order to produce more
quickly something you want, subject it to an inconceivably
horrible existence, even inject stuff into it and make it a sort of
top-heavy, grotesque figure – that is not respecting human
life.

And I'll tell you exactly what will happen, though you
won't believe me. What will happen will be that, in so far as
the argument is employed that it is legitimate to do this
because for economic reasons it makes it easier for us to live in
the way we wish to live, the same argument will in time be
applied to men. If you say you can get more out of a chicken in
a broiler-house, therefore it's legitimate to have a broiler-
house, so someone will say, and it has already been said in
many cases, that if you put men into broiler-houses you'll get
more work out of them and they'll be more malleable. And so
our very society will turn into a broiler-house, and in fact it is
rapidly so turning at this moment.

In December 1980 a team which also included Enoch Powell was asked to express its views on blood sports.

I don't personally regard anti-blood sports as a very important cause, although I must say, seeing a lot of grown-up people on horses, with dogs chasing a fox...

POWELL: *Hounds, please.*

... is, of course, pretty silly; but compared with the appalling things that are done to animals in what is called factory farming, heartily disgusting things which were responsible for my becoming a vegetarian, I don't take it too seriously.

I think that the use of animals recklessly, on a large scale, for human purposes and for vivisection and all these different things, is a very ominous sign of the present state of our society, and that in the future we shall find that by relaxing every sort of concern for animals, except a utilitarian one, we shall land ourselves in becoming very what's called 'animal' in our ways.

FIFTEEN

Miscellaneous

In March 1957 a team which included Lady Barnett, who was at that time advertising tea bags, was asked whether it was right for public personalities to lend their names to commercial advertising campaigns, and could they do so with any sincerity.

I don't see why they shouldn't lend their names to commercial advertising campaigns provided they are paid adequately, and as for the question of sincerity, of course sincerity is a very tricky and dangerous word. I daresay it may well be that most of them manage to persuade themselves, at any rate for a little while, that what they say about this or that commodity they really do mean. I can't see any objection to it.

I only hope they don't suffer the fate of a friend of mine who was at the other end of the thing and was writing advertising copy for patent medicines, and this unhappy man had to give it up because he found that by writing this advertising copy he was developing all the complaints. Having been a perfectly healthy man, he became acid and flat-footed, and I hope that one of the hazards of recommending these things is not that you develop the complaints that they're supposed to cure.

Don't forget that it is not any new development. I mean, all we poor hack reviewers, we've been grinding out recommendations for books for years and years and years.

How often I've written in a ghastly notice of a book, 'I could not lay it down', and then tried to salvage my conscience by having a picture of myself with it sort of stuck to my hands.

Malcolm was less tolerant about advertising in June 1963 when a questioner asked if there was too much licence in advertising.

Well, obviously most advertising is lies, isn't it? By the nature of the case, if you're going to advertise, recommend it to someone, it's almost certain that you'll exaggerate its qualities and therefore ninety per cent of advertising is lies. And it is very cleverly put out, which you induce people to believe. I think this is a pretty deplorable state of affairs.

I think the effect of advertising on our society in every way, including a great deal of stimulating of desires for things that people don't really want, is one of its most pernicious elements. If, on the other hand, you say to me, 'How can you protect the public from this, short of just banning advertising as is done in Communist countries?'.... It's one of the few, to me, rather pleasing aspects of a Communist country that there is no advertising except, of course, of the regime, which is pretty boring. So I would say in answer to this question, yes, there is far too much licence in advertising and increasingly so, but it is extremely difficult to see how, in a society of our kind, it's possible to protect the public against it.

About making them sceptical at school and so on, I'm very doubtful about the efficacy of that because the public is undoubtedly getting more and more gullible, as you can see from the nature of the advertising which is put out, despite the fact that more and more money is spent on education. Take, for instance, detergent advertising. Everybody knows these detergents are exactly the same: same product, same chemical composition. Now, millions are spent on advertising them. As a journalist I, in a minute way, participate in those millions, so in taking this position I'm really going against my own interest. But the point is that it's a total and utter waste, and the claims that are made for them, for these identical substances, have to become more and more untrue, so that the whole effect on society of this idiotic activity, putting over on people things which are palpably false, cannot but in my opinion be bad.

You see it in America, where you see it to the ultimate extent, when some of the best brains, some of the best endeavour in the country, are being devoted solely to persuading people to want what they don't want, to get rid of things before they're worn out, to buy other things that are totally unnecessary; and it's only by all that activity that this mad society can run.

In May 1966 a questioner asked: 'To write a good novel do you require a little knowledge and a vast imagination or a vast knowledge and a little imagination?'

As a hater of facts, a man who believes that the whole twentieth century has been poisoned by obsession with facts, most of which are phoney, I naturally am on the side of imagination. There was a French novelist I daresay none of you have had the misfortune to read called Zola, who specialised in facts – the greatest bore who ever lived. Whereas, of course, *Wuthering Heights*, that contained absolutely no facts – and in so far as there are any they're wrong – is a great work of genius.

If I was a praying man, which unfortunately I'm not, I

should pray to be delivered from facts, and I'm sure that when our civilisation finally sinks and the waves close over its head, it will be because it's stuffed stupified with facts; so that the novels that evade facts, to my taste, are infinitely superior.

Tolstoy's facts, of course, were all wrong; he was a very good novelist. Dostoievsky's facts weren't even apparently right; he was a very good novelist. Most modern novelists write entirely about sex and I like to think that their facts are wrong.

In November 1967 the programme visited the Northcott Theatre in Exeter and a questioner asked whether the running expenses of theatres such as that one should be subsidised annually by local councils. The team also included Ted Willis and Rosamund John, the former actress, who were both strongly in favour. Rosamund John said that the uneasy attitude towards local councils subsidising the theatre in our day was very similar to the attitude that prevailed much earlier in the century towards libraries; while Ted Willis referred to the old Chinese proverb that if you're starving and somebody gives you two pennies, you should spend one penny on food and one penny on a bunch of hyacinths.

May I point out to you the exquisite humour of Ted referring to the sort of plays that are going to be put on in this delightful theatre as hyacinths. I mean, if you look at some of the plays that have been put on in London by subsidised theatres – that wonderful Sade play when you have all the blue blood squirting on the stage – not much of a hyacinth, that particular one.

Of course I accept Miss John's very charming plea for this, but at the same time there is an awful lot of humbug in it. First of all, the comparison with libraries is totally phoney. Because, you see, a library, without any great expense, can cater for practically every taste, whereas if you get a theatre like this it will be run by a rather highbrow director and I know exactly the plays he will put on. It's absolutely inevitable. I can see him, I can see his beard, I know everything about him – I can tell you the plays without the slightest difficulty.

Now, the notion that dear Miss John has that working men are going to crowd in here to see these plays – dismiss it from your mind. I'll give you five pounds for every working man who voluntarily comes into this theatre. Poor Arnold Wesker, bless his heart, good man, true man, he's been trying to do this. He's had the idea that the trade unionists should have a marvellous theatre but, of course, their ideas of the theatre and Wesker's are completely different.

Now I'm sure that in this rich town with many public-spirited citizens the amount that you'll pay for this theatre is trivial. But I would suggest to you there is an awful lot of cant in this; that things that are subsidised – whether they're admirable or not is a matter of taste and opinion – are in fact things for a minority, and a very small minority, and, what is more, a minority that could perfectly well afford to pay for them themselves.

Malcolm appeared in an unfamiliar role, that of an economist, in November 1968. The question was: 'Too many people have too much spare cash; imports go up, the country is in the red – what should be done about it?'

Ever since I can remember, year by year, I have been told by those who sit in authority over me that we are bust, that our economic affairs are in a hopeless confusion, that an economic and financial crisis is just round the corner, that there is a flight from the pound – although my trouble's always been a flight to it, really – and that we must tighten our belts. This has been going on for years. We haven't ever balanced our budget in my living memory – nor, as far as I know, has any country in the Western world – so I can only suppose that in some extraordinary way, if we go on in this crazy manner, nothing will happen to us.

It's all very extraordinary, of course. I mean, for instance, take the attitude to the pound sterling. We've made the pound into a sort of person. We say, 'The pound had a good day yesterday.' The pound was able to sit up and take a little nourishment. I find it very baffling.

Thanks to the enlightened Labour Government that we've had for the past four years, we are so much in debt that we can never possibly pay it back, and therefore it will be to the interest of everybody else to keep us going.

One would not have expected Malcolm to be very enthusiastic about the Concorde project. Nor was he, and when in January 1976 there was a question about Bishop Hugh Montefiore's speech in New York where he was critical of Concorde, Malcolm spoke up for the Bishop.

I have thought from the beginning that it was a most ludicrous enterprise in which to sink this vast amount of money, and I don't agree that when something is done of which you disapprove you are necessarily knocking your country in an unfair way if you draw attention to it. A great many things have been done in the last fifty years that I've had the misfortune to observe, public affairs which I've disapproved of, and I can't believe that in expressing that feeling I was damaging it.

I think it was a great pity we ever started on Concorde. I think when it runs it will be a flop, because it can't carry enough passengers; the whole enterprise is a lamentable one. The idea that making an aeroplane faster and faster and faster is necessarily progress is one of the great fantasies of the twentieth century and one of the things that serve to make life increasingly disagreeable for everybody concerned. The advantage of being able to cross the Atlantic and save three hours is absolutely minimal, and I'm delighted to think that the number of people who will be imbecile enough to pay the very high fares on this plane is strictly limited.

In May 1980 the team was asked: 'What, if any, are the advantages of growing old?'

The advantages are colossal. Everybody here can look forward eagerly to getting into their late seventies, which is what I am now. First of all, you get rid of an enormous amount of junk. You get rid of ambition – what a boring thing that is. You don't totally get rid of lechery; you get rid of a good solid part of it, which is very excellent. You have a most delightful feeling of irresponsibility; so, for instance, you might open *The Times* – the most boring newspaper ever known to man – and you see in it an enormous article, we'll say on the Channel Tunnel, and you say to yourself, 'I needn't read it, because the Channel Tunnel does not affect me in any way.' So you're let off an enormous amount of tedious reading, tedious talk.

And this is the funny thing about it, and I'm being very serious, two points: one is that you have, strangely enough, an additional, sharpened sense of what a delightful place the world is and how enchanting are your fellow human beings. Quite illogical in a way – maybe it's just because you're going to leave them – but still you have that feeling.

And secondly, which is perhaps the most agreeable of all – I've got nine grandchildren, and I find their company absolutely enchanting. Whether that's because I am rapidly relapsing into second childhood and so I'm at one with them, or whether it's just a feeling that they're beginning this pilgrimage through the world and I'm just ending it, but it is the most delightful experience. So whatever you do, get some grandchildren, and you'll be all right.